A
PASSION
FOR CARS

From his earliest years Anthony Gibbs has
lived in thrall to motorcars. For him they
have been objects of love and empathy,
creations to be judged on their elegance,
distinction and personality. His nostalgia
for the pre-war vintages of the twenties and
thirties—the Delages, Rolls-Royces and
Daimlers (to name but a few)—is insepar-
able from the adventures and delights he
shared with his four-wheeled mistresses.
With an accomplished and witty style the
author uses the medium of his cars to take
us on a lighthearted and cosmopolitan tour
of his life. His 'passion' was first nurtured
by his mother in the days when a car was
bought to be rebuilt to one's taste. And
from then onwards he never looked back—
he has personally owned forty-seven cars.
Each has its own anecdotes and history,
whether in England, France, Germany or
America; each has its place in his career as
writer, publisher and family man.
To complement the author's nostalgic
reminiscences there is a large selection of
illustrations evoking the motoring days of
style and glamour, now lost for ever.

ANTHONY GIBBS

A PASSION FOR CARS

CHARLES SCRIBNER'S SONS
NEW YORK

ACKNOWLEDGEMENTS: The publishers would like to thank the following for their permission to reproduce the illustrations in this book: Montagu Motor Museum, London Express News and Feature Service, Radio Times Hulton Picture Library, Renault, Vauxhall Motors, British Motor Corporation, Popperfoto, Daily Telegraph Colour Library and Punch

First published in 1974 by
David & Charles (Holdings) Limited England

Printed in Great Britain

Library of Congress Catalog Card Number 73-11587

SBN 684-13636-8 (cloth)

Contents

CHAPTER I

The
Family
Influence

THE FIRST CAR I had anything to do with was a
quivering, shaking, revolting machine called the
Jigger. I have no idea who manufactured the thing,
but it was owned by an uncle of mine who was a
bacteriologist at the Lister Institute, at the corner of
Chelsea Bridge.

It was a tricycle with the single wheel at the back.
This had an enormous single cylinder attached, more
or less directly, to the hub. Just in front of that, on a
saddle, sat my uncle in a sheepskin coat, with his cap
turned the wrong way round and a pair of frightening
goggles over his eyes.

1

In front of that was a very large wicker basket shaped
so that two people could sit in it, and my uncle would
steer the machine by aiming his passengers in the
general direction in which he wanted to go. It was more
than a little alarming to occupy this position, for the
curl or lip one rested one's feet up on was only about
three inches above the surface of the road, so that it
seemed very intimate indeed, as did any obstacle such
as a large, stationary dray with a pissing horse from
which one would be swerved away at what seemed the
last possible moment.

I don't imagine that any of these contrivances have
survived into modern times, though I seem to remember that a commercial variant could be seen in
the more opulent streets of London until the coming of
the First World War. These had a definite elegance.
The basket was supplanted by a neat square box
positioned between the two front wheels, with rather
superior names painted thereon, like 'Worth' or
'Fortnum and Mason'. If the chauffeur was smartly
dressed with a peaked cap and a well-cut overcoat
with a fur collar, the effect was quite impressive.

Another uncle of mine, who married the illegitimate
daughter of a certain duke, was the possessor of an
Argyll. This would have been about 1910. It was very
tall, and there was a great deal of gleaming brass,
enormous lamps and one of those strange windscreens
that ascended in a controllable zig-zag, each section
provided with a knurled nut and little brass teeth to
fix it in any desired position.

I thought it was rather a splendid motorcar. To get
into it you climbed up a staircase at the back, opened a
door, painted green with red lines, and found yourself
in 'the tonneau' with a marvellous view over the
hedges. The tonneau had buttoned upholstery more or

less all over it, and its corners were rounded, so that you could sit half-sideways, with your legs crossed and one arm over the edge, very comfortably indeed.

Down below, in front, was the driving compartment. This had a perfectly vertical dashboard of polished wood rising from the floor, and all over it were rows of gleaming brass 'oilers'. These had a glass tube through which you could see the oil actually pouring down in a thin stream to all the places that needed it, like the engine bearings and one thing and another; and before starting the engine you had to turn on all the little brass taps and be quite certain that, from that moment until you switched off with a cough and a sigh, not one of them failed to function. Because if one of them did you were in big trouble.

The Argyll, I remember well, had very good manners, but I cannot recall its ever completing a journey. My uncle never travelled without a large enamel bowl, for collecting essential juices, a large bucket of water, and a small boy, the gardener's son, to go for help in the event of trouble.

You stood beside the machine, leaned over, set the hand throttle, and the mixture control, and the ignition advance, all on a quadrant in the middle of the steering wheel, to the positions long experience had taught you. Incidentally, there was a bulb-horn also attached to the underneath of that steering wheel. This was perfectly convenient for the straight ahead position, but in moments of emergency when a sharp pull on the wheel became necessary, I've seen my uncle diving after that thing like a cormorant in search of a fish.

To resume. You then strolled to the front of the car, took the starting handle out of its leather strap, slotted it in, pulled it, quite gently, over one compression, and the engine started, almost silently. My 3 uncle then clambered in, taking care not to get the outside gear lever or the brake up the leg of his trousers, the small boy leaped in beside him, the ladies in the tonneau tugged at the knots of their veils, and away we went.

The roads in those days were all white, covered in two or three inches of dust, and as the Argyll proceeded smoothly on its way it disturbed this and threw it up behind in a great mushroom cloud which blotted out the landscape for miles behind, so that it took perhaps ten minutes before it settled back on the blackberry hedges and the surface of the road, so that all was clean again. Perhaps this was one of the things which made the motorcar unpopular.

In a very gentlemanly and dignified manner, when everybody was expecting it, the Argyll would quietly come to rest. Without swearing at all, my uncle would thumb up each end of his moustache. The small boy dismounted, lay on the road, and examined the under-neath of the car.

'Anything?'

'No, sir!'

'Have a look at the water.'

He had a look at the water.

'There isn't any, sir.'

'None at all?'

'No, sir.'

'Well, what about the bucket?'

'Must have dropped off, sir.'

My uncle made that little gesture with his moustache again. He was a very handsome man.

'Cut back then!'

'Very good, sir!'

The small boy disappeared into the dust, and a great silence fell, except for the little noises of the countryside. The birds twittered in the trees. From somewhere came the sound of water lapping over stones.

My uncle took the enamel bowl and went through a gate into a field, which was full of buttercups and cows. In ten minutes or so he came back with the bowl full of water. He poured this into the radiator and disappeared again. In about five minutes the sound of water leaking from the radiator ceased. In ten my uncle was back again with another bowl.

It was about an hour later that the small boy returned, riding upon a horse.

After that there was a war, and in a very short time there was no motoring, unless you could get somebody to fit one of those gasbags to the roof of the car, and adapt the carburettor to fit. You really only saw those in the region of Park Lane. But the moment the war was over the family bought a car and engaged an ex-service man to drive it. His name was Arthur.

The car was an Iris Landaulette. It was, of course, a pre-war model, very square and upright, like a private taxi. It had a silly little four-cylinder engine and a right-hand change with four ratios. It needed four. Its radiator was a close copy of the contemporary Fiat, tapering inwards towards the top, and I *think* it bore a trefoil device, like the wearing of the green. Inside was rather grubby Bedford Cord. The windows had tatty embroidered straps to pull them up. If you wanted them down you made use of the force of gravity. The door handles were mother-of-pearl.

It was an extremely boring and pedestrian motorcar, and while my father was away somewhere, my mother, who was showing early symptoms of motormania, swapped it for an Austin Twenty. Another landaulette.

This wasn't the post-war, slightly Americanized Austin Twenty with the painted radiator. This one was all brass, with the squarish, rounded radiator carrying the famous Austin emblem of two wings sprouting from a wheel.

Its main impression on my youthful mind, apart from the twenty horsepower, and the extraordinary, dungeon-like cold of its interior, was that its petrol was fed by pressure. The tank was at the back, which was considered in those days to be distinctly upper class. Daimlers and Rollses *always* had their tanks at the back, generally with a large glass gauge so that you could see at a glance how much was in it.

Daimlers, of course, had those protective wooden slats, which really was a piece of one-upmanship over the Rolls itself. The effect of this pressure arrangement was that Arthur was provided in front with a brass pump that looked remarkably like a fire extinguisher, with a handle and a plunger. It was low down, somewhere near the floor, so that he had to bend over sideways to work it.

I am not at all certain, but I imagine the intention was that, once the tank had been pumped up with thirty or forty strokes and the engine had started, the pressure was to become self-perpetuating. If so, the system didn't work. Huddled in overcoats and rugs in the dark body of the machine, my mother and I, every twenty seconds or so, would see Arthur, on the other side of his glass, in a state of convulsive sideways activity, pumping up the juice. This reduced us on our first few runs through the streets of London to helpless laughter, but it very soon became annoying.

One day, when my father was away in America describing the condition of Germany after the defeat, the Austin was persuaded to trundle all the way to

6

Bexhill. Arthur tottered from the driving seat with a white face streaming with perspiration.

Obviously something had to be done. At some sort of tea party we met a man who had a showroom near Leicester Square, in which stood a six-cylinder Buick. Just the car, he said, for us. Wouldn't we like to see it? He could easily telephone to London and have it brought down.

The very next morning the Buick stood outside the Sackville Hotel. It was a grey open tourer with the rather tinny American looks of the period. The radiator was painted and the body had obviously, except for the doors, been stamped out of one piece. It had wooden wheels with 'demountable rims' and the spare demountable rim was a recognizable feature of the back. The whole machine sloped upwards in a way about which the Americans didn't seem to worry for the next twenty years, so that the gap between the rear wheel and the wing was twice that in front. Apart from this it was not unshapely, having a flowing line quite foreign to the stodgy English designs.

It had other things which were foreign. It had an electric self-starter, six-volt battery ignition, and a dynamo. It had six cylinders, and overhead valves. And it had, to Arthur's amazement, a whippy gear lever sticking straight up from the gear-box in the middle of the floor, with only three gears to its name.

We got in. It was a bitterly cold morning, but we dismissed offers of the cape-carthood and celluloid curtains. The starter engaged with rather an unenthusiastic whine, the engine hissed with a complete absence of vibration, in went second gear, and we surged away at about 36 mph without a sound.

That was a very good car. Once top gear was engaged 7

it was never—literally never—necessary to change again unless one came to an absolute stop. And even then a delicate foot on the clutch pedal was enough to get the Buick moving again without a murmur of protest. We whistled into St Leonards, swooped up all the hills, fled round all the corners, and arrived back at the hotel, exhilarated, amazed, and blue with cold.

We said it was marvellous, fantastic, a revelation, but what did we do about that cold?

Mr Le Francois said he thought the car really deserved a special body.

'Special body?' my mother echoed, her eyes alight.

Mr Le Francois knew a very good, old-established firm called Alexander's, of Clapham. They were very accustomed to submit designs to customers' requirements, build them by craftsmen, and it wouldn't, he thought, cost more than about £350.

This was enough for my mother, and to be quite honest, it was enough for me. I have always taken a passionate and, I hope, intelligent interest in the shapes of cars. I had even evolved certain rules, which I think still hold. All horizontal lines should either be horizontal, or slope or curve downwards towards the back. The windscreen should occur exactly at the halfway point between the axles, and the roof should come down exactly over the rear axle. There are others, but I'll come to those later.

We had a very happy time in the purlieus of Clapham and I'm afraid I opted for a two-door, four-window, drophead saloon. While we waited for the body to be built we found that all the Austin needed was a new washer somewhere along the line, and I acquired my very own first car.

It was a 1914 Standard Nine open two-seater. A squat, solid, unimaginative little thing, the precise opposite in conception to the Buick. I think it cost £45.

It had the old, very vertical Standard radiator done in brass with a very large Union Jack. I'm not sure that there weren't Union Jacks on the wheel-hubs as well. The wheels were the conventional Sankey steel Artillery. Very spidery. I never fell in love with it, but I was waiting to go up to Oxford at the time, and it gave me my freedom and got me about very unobtrusively to places like the Hammersmith Palais de Danse, and the Royal Academy of Music, where I was filling in time by taking a course in harmony. In those days there were so few cars about that you simply drove up to a place, pulled on the handbrake, got out and went in.

I had to crank it, of course, and I have no idea at what speed it went because it didn't have a speedo-meter, the gear-change was, naturally, in a gate on the right, and the clutch was so heavy that, if you wanted to go, say, from third into top, you had to count ten before you could think of putting it in. One thing it did have was an extra air valve worked by a knurled knob on the steering wheel. This set up a tremendous hissing which made passers-by turn their heads. This was my chief memory of that little car, of tooling along the empty roads at about twenty-five miles an hour with that supersonic whistle just under one's face.

In those days Oxford undergraduates weren't allowed to have cars in their first year, so I sold it and bought an A.V. Monocar.

The great advantage of the A.V., apart from the fact that it was a most excellent machine, was its extreme narrowness. It can't have been much more than eighteen inches wide, though it was all of ten or eleven feet long.

This one was painted blue. It went to a sharp point

in front so you could have a good view of the bobbin
steering. This was swung around a central pivot by
steel wires attached to the steering wheel. This
particular Monocar was very second hand, and I have
known the wheels make a full turn of 180° and carry on,
which was disconcerting, if you weren't expecting it.

Anyhow, there was a single seat about halfway along,
the gears were ex-flivver, down for bottom, up for top,
and somewhere in the middle for neutral, and there
was a hand throttle attached to the vehicle's side. In
front of you were an 'aero' screen and two splendid
Grebel searchlights, while behind was a perfectly
naked V-twin Jap engine sticking out, which made the
air boil and seethe when it got really hot.

I made a working arrangement with a sweet shop
in the Broad to keep this invention in their front
passage. I would then saunter negligently into the
shop, purchase a small bag of acid drops, pass through
a side door, turn on the petrol, tickle the carburettor,
and pull about one and a half yards of chain out of the
machinery. The engine spat with a lusty beat, I
emerged at speed, and ho! for the Riviera Hotel at
Maidenhead, where there was always a chance of seeing
Gladys Cooper.

The trouble with the Grebels was that they worked
off a rather elderly battery which was innocent of any
dynamo. Coming back from Maidenhead in the dark
behind two half-mile beams, I would become aware of
their intensity gradually reducing itself to a feeble
glimmer, which made it difficult to see, unless there
was a moon. Driving through Dorchester one evening
and trying to pick out the general direction of the road
I was suddenly confronted with a forest of legs at
impossible angles, rather like the crest of the Isle of
Man. A complete Mormon street meeting leapt to

safety and I passed through to a chorus of yells, but without touching a single trouser.

After this I made representations to my mother, and she came up with a perfectly new scarlet Monocar, from somewhere just behind Bond Street. I often wonder whether it is the one which now graces Lord Montagu of Beaulieu's museum, and I cannot imagine why somebody does not manufacture something very similar today. For one person wanting to get about by himself in complete comfort it was ideal. It slid through the traffic like a scooter, and with 800 cc. in that Jap and a front end you could lift with one finger, its performance was fantastic. I have no idea how fast it went because it didn't possess a speedometer, but there was one place on the road between Maidenhead and Henley which I used to take at what must have been a cool seventy, because I habitually became airborne for a considerable number of yards.

In the meantime, that Buick had turned up with its new body. Aesthetically it was not markedly successful. It still sloped up towards the back. It still had those ridged American mudguards which were obviously the child of the giant press rather than the affectionate skill of the panel beater. And stuck behind it still had that spindly demountable rim with a worn tyre and a lot of rusty lugs.

Added to this the giant oaken beams and quarter-inch-thick plate glass considered necessary in a gentleman's carriage by our good friends in Clapham had reduced the performance of those six cylinders, with their push-rod overhead valves, to the merely nice-mannered normal.

One day, when my father was away again and my attention was otherwise engaged, my mother and

Arthur sneaked off together to a motor showroom in
Upper Regent Street, where my mother went completely mad and wrote them a cheque for £2,300. I
suppose you could multiply that by about six today.

The result of this escapade was that, at about half-
past five that evening as I looked out of the window, a
gigantic Daimler radiator, fully five feet from the
ground, steamed into view. About twelve feet behind
this sat our Arthur with a broad grin on his face. Then
a series of windows passed in review, and, minutes
later, as it seemed, the rear of the vehicle hove in sight.

That really was a fantastic motorcar. It was called
the Daimler Special Forty-five. It had a six-cylinder
sleeve-valve engine of seven litres, which was utterly
silent and did exactly nine miles to the gallon. Even
service stations were rocked when it drove up to the
hand-cranked pump and Arthur said, 'Forty-five
gallons, please!'

It had a nine-seater cabriolet body by Salmons of
really cavernous proportions, and the whole equipage
was gleaming with nickel-plate and royal blue paint,
and a black leather top. I have no idea how on earth
that top was arranged to be put down. I don't believe
we ever tried. There were three rows of seats in all
of which you could stretch your legs, so that the effect,
if you looked through the windscreen, was rather like a
quick peep into the Albert Hall. Where all that leather
went beggars the imagination. I seem to remember
from various eyelets and things at the back of the
car that you were supposed to furl it like a sail and fix
it with straps.

That car would climb the steepest hill you could
present it with, at six miles an hour in top gear, in
utter quiet. On the other hand, its absolute maximum
12 was exactly 50 mph. All the sleeve-valve Daimlers were

like that, even the magnificent Double Six. Impressive smoothness up to fifty, after which all the toggles and sleeves and pistons fought to jump out of the car. It didn't matter much. In those days nobody wanted to drive at 50 mph. We only tried it once, and all the people in the middle row hit their heads on one of the cross-pieces of the roof, so that there was bedlam and quite a bit of blood to be got off the Bedford Cord upholstery with cold water.

Normally, in those days, the traffic, in so far as there was any traffic, moved at precisely 30 mph, out of deference to the 20 mph speed limit. Police traps were the order of the day—the most famous of them was between the two bridges coming out of Kingston on the Portsmouth Road, and the A.A. bombarded its members with the slogan 'If the A.A. scout fails to salute, stop and ask the reason why'.

At this speed the Special Forty-five sailed along like the *Queen Mary*, with the hedgerows and things quietly slipping past all the windows, the only sound that splendid whine of the old square-cut Dunlop tyres which was one of the nicest noises in motoring, especially when, with a fastish car, it rose to an exhilarating scream.

At about this time I came down from Oxford rather abruptly and went with my father to America. He was on a lecture tour. This must have been in 1921, and America was still a railway civilization. Each town we went to seemed to be an all-night journey from the next. The trains were marvellously well-arranged. From the moment you crawled out of a taxi at the station, and your luggage was seized by a cheerful 'red-cap', you never had to bother with it again until you arrived at the other end and found another red-cap waiting with it at the open door of a cab. In the

13

meantime you had dined admirably and slept in your
private 'drawing-room', while the vast engine ploughed
through the night, its bell ringing, its headlamp
blazing the way ahead, and its whistle rising and
falling in major thirds. There was the romance of
steam in all that.

Except for Moscow, and they do say Siberia,
America has the worst climate in the world. New York
has a temperature range of one hundred degrees, all the
way from the hundred to zero. A lot of it is more dram-
atic than that. In the Middle West with a touch of
North, the inhabitants are perfectly accustomed to
'thirty below' or even 'forty below', which means 72°
of frost.

As an Englishman who faints in a heat-wave of 75°
or freezes to death at 33°, I found the whole situation
intolerable. This was mid-winter, and the way in
which the comfort-loving American, who would call
to the train porter, 'Can't somebody get a bit of heat
into this car?' when the inside temperature was already 80° in the shade, could endure driving about in
an open tourer with flapping side-screens passed
comprehension.

There were many kind people who met us at the
places where my father had the next lecture booked,
and we would step out of that summer heat and go
clanking off into the snow, to arrive almost dead with
exposure. Yet, apart from the taxis, I don't remember
seeing a single closed car anywhere in the country,
except in New York where a few rich people ran
Rolls-Royces, or could afford to pay someone like Le
Baron to construct them a 'custom sedan'.

That was the year when Dodge, greatly daring and
much applauded, first put a standard sedan on the
assembly line.

All the same quite a metamorphosis had taken place
in those American towns since the day our old Buick
was made. It is true the radiators were still painted
and the wings were still stamped out in presses, but
an enormous improvement in their lines had given
them an appearance of luxury and thrust. Long high
bonnets and low stubby seating matched the American
automobile to the impressiveness of the American
locomotive. Does anybody remember the names?
the Apperson Beauty Eight; the Cole Aero Eight; the
Paige; the Templar; that very good car the Marmon;
the Locomobile, with ugly froglamps on its wings; the
Packard; the Packard Twin-Six. Only the Cadillac
is still with us, sliding nobly, as it did then, through a
shoal of Fords, Chevrolets, and Dodges.

All these big powerful machines were built to the
same ideal: 'From Two to Eighty in High'.

In my opinion this was the right ideal. The modern
motorway trend of five gears, with, possibly, a couple
of overdrives on top of that, has arisen simply because
the European manufacturer will persist in trying to
get too much out of too small an engine. Taxation?
Something niggling in his nature? I don't know. At the
moment I am running a second-hand car which will
go from zero to 124 mph without a change of gear,
out-accelerating the gear-twiddlers all the way. I
believe they only sold 900.

It's strange, isn't it? In 1921 the world was popu-
lated with millions of Tin Lizzies, all functioning
perfectly satisfactorily on two gears, just like my
Monocar.

The Monocar went. When we got back from
America I fell romantically in love, and though the
young lady in question (we didn't call them girl-
friends in those days. Well, they weren't, were they?)

was awfully nice about it and quite prepared to perch
on a little folding seat I had rigged up between me and
the Jap, I really wanted room for two.

So I invested in an Amilcar. That was a distinctly
elegant little machine, with nice looks and a beautifully
balanced engine of 1087 cc. The original Riley Nine,
also of 1087 cc., was the sincerest form of flattery.
With its high prow and the word Amilcar so correctly
offset, its wire wheels and its engine-turned dashboard, it was as pretty as a picture and as sweet as a
Singer sewing machine. The family had moved to the
neighbourhood of Dorking, and as it was always rain-
ing I bought it a screen wiper. This consisted simply
of a clip lined with crêpe rubber. You slipped it over
the top of the windscreen like a clothes peg, and pushed
it about. It wasn't very satisfactory, but at least it was
better than the half potato which many people carried.

I also bought it a hard top. I think this must have
been the first hard top ever invented, forty-five years
ahead of the fashion. There was a chap in Battersea
who advertised in the motor papers what he called a
'coupé top', and I hied off to see him. It was simply a
wood frame covered in a tarpaulin-type material. Unfortunately the Amilcar had very rudimentary doors.
In fact it only had one, about eight inches deep. The
other side was masked by the spare wheel. The polite
drill was to open the eight inches gallantly for the lady,
swing the handle *en passant*, and vault into the driver's
seat with a flash of suède shoe and purple socks.

So we had to be still more inventive. We came up
with the idea of putting the whole thing on a hinge at
the back, and rigging up a species of pole in front.

When the car was being driven this pole was kept
flat against the roof by spring clips. When you wanted
16 to alight you grabbed the thing, unclipped it, and began

paying it upwards like punting on the river Cher. After a bit the roof, opening like the wings of a gigantic beetle, would go over top-dead-centre and flop down to the slope of the boot.

This always fetched a crowd, which I found embarrassing. It also entirely spoiled the lines of the Amilcar. The chap hadn't put enough struts in the centre so that the blessed contraption dished, looking almost as unpleasant as the same treatment on a Mercedes. Also the leathercloth and the tall side-windows looked cheap and nasty. So I sold the Amilcar and bought a real, honest-to-God coupé.

It was a Mathis. The streets of Paris in those days were rippling with fastidious little coupés, many with carriage-lamps and other touches of *panache*, and this Mathis was the most fastidious of the lot. It had been brought to this country by the great M. Weymann himself, who had, as I'm sure you know, developed a new system of flexible material. So this was the first Weymann body ever to cross the Channel.

To look at, it was a little darling, with basketwork to the waistline, and a very square, shiny black top and bonnet. It had Michelin disc wheels, elaborately ringed in ivory, carriage lamps, and an electrical self-starter. It had one extraordinarily comfortable seat upholstered in grey cloth, like a drawing-room sofa, and to travel in it was to be pervaded by a sense of fashion and luxury.

Like all the little French cars of the period, except the Citroëns, its engine spun like a top. But it was tiny. On the level or downhill it would travel with silence and quite a bit of speed; but the slightest adverse gradient would send one's hand to the chunky gear-lever. Fortunately it possessed that rarity, a multiplate clutch.

17

The effect of this was to cut out any need for double-declutching. The trick was to keep the accelerator on the floor and slip the plates. This speeded up the engine without speeding up the gear-box, and when you got the feel of it the lower gear sidled in like a spinster into church.

I had acquired a job in a grisly thoroughfare known as Farringdon Street, and I used my little Mathis for commuting. Every day we slipped through Dorking, Leatherhead, Ashtead, Epsom, Wimbledon, Putney Bridge, and along the Embankment all the way to Blackfriars. The Managing Director of this enormous concern, Sir George Something-or-other, was the only other man who had a car. He always arrived earlier than I did, and left his car bang in the middle of the road. I would slink to a dainty stop behind him.

After about a year of this Sir George began to show signs of curiosity, and when his enquiries uncovered the fact that the owner was the lowliest worker in the place, he sent for me and expressed resentment and distaste. He made it clear that if I wanted to keep my job, the only thing to do was to abandon the Mathis; on the other hand, if I wanted to use my Mathis, the only thing to do was to resign the job, which I accordingly did.

That wasn't the only great change in life. The whole thing was occasioned by my mother, who had a mania for changing houses only equalled by her passion for changing cars.

It was decided that I could be given a year in which to try my hand at writing a book. My father had also abandoned his journalism and was grinding out a book a year, punctuated by lecture tours in the United States. This reduced the proximity of Dorking Station to complete unimportance. My mother had

long been thinking that the neighbourhood was
rapidly acquiring the ambience of outer suburbia, and
she had discovered a really very beautiful house, in
real country, overlooking Cuttmill pond, which one
got to by going from Guildford along the Hog's Back.

My father saw his chance and took it. He had long
been nagging about the Daimler, which, he said, gave
people false ideas. He now announced that it would use
a gallon and a half of petrol every time he wanted to
post a letter. He said he would buy the house only if
she agreed to sell the Daimler.

My mother, near to tears, sacked the faithful Arthur,
and went to see Mr Le Francois. He recommended a
monstrous machine called a Métallurgique.

This Métallurgique was a handsome beast, about the
size of the largest Rolls, and with a radiator distinctly
reminiscent of the Rolls, except that it sloped back
on either side to form a neat V. Rather an improvement if anything. But, my goodness, it was a banger.
Under that imposing bonnet were four iron cylinders
of phenomenal stroke, and the gears, if you were
strong enough and ruthless enough to mesh their giant
cogs, were so high that each explosion was a sledge-
hammer blow. My mother couldn't even get it out of
the drive. So she went back to Mr Le Francois.

Mr Le Francois pointed out, quite kindly, that the
car was now second-hand so that there would be a
drop in value. He admitted that it wasn't really a lady's
car, being designed for the long straight roads of
Belgium. But he had just the very thing for her ladyship.
A *small* Métallurgique, of only eighteen horsepower.

My mother brightened. It happened to be in the
showroom. It had the same radiator, nice lines, those
Americanized wire wheels with a complicated spoke-
pattern, it gleamed, and Mr Le Francois suggested

that we drive it down to Cuttmill to see how we liked it.

So we got aboard, the starter whirred, the bottom gear found itself engaged, and we emerged, with the engine roaring, at precisely 1 mph.

That car was the exact opposite of its elder brother. The gears were so low that at any perceptible speed the four cylinders ran out of revs. They also vibrated savagely. Everything in the neat, blue leather interior set up a sympathetic buzz, tinkle, rattle or boom. To touch any part of the metal was to receive a perfect imitation of an electric shock from an alternating current. We arrived home with blinding headaches. My mother rang up Mr Le Francois. She said it felt like being in an iron cage. Mr Le Francois suggested an open four-seater Citroën.

He explained, kindly, that the arithmetic was getting rather complicated, but he was prepared to take the Daimler in part exchange for the first Métallurgique, the first in part exchange for the second, the second in part exchange for the Citroën, if milady would make up the difference of £130.

So we had a Citroën.

The first time we went out, with my mother driving, we had a distinguished passenger in the rear seat who wanted to be driven to church. That is to say my mother wanted to go to church and insisted that A. S. M. Hutchinson, who had just written a book called *If Winter Comes*, must come as well. As we were approaching Effingham my mother drove straight up a tree. The car stopped at an angle of not more than five degrees from the vertical, and A.S.M. found himself sliding, gently but irresistibly, out of the back seat on to a mossy bank. He survived.

That Citroën was the first French version of the new
20   international trend, a mass-produced vehicle a cut

above the Tin Lizzy, and selling at a price about half
as much again. The English equivalent was, of course,
the bull-nosed Morris Cowley, and the American, the
Chevrolet. It had a four-cylinder engine of 11.9
horse-power, a central gear-change mounted on a ball,
and Chevron gears in the back axle which may or may
not have produced a sensuous quiet, but certainly became the badge motif of the marque.

As I have mentioned, the accent in those days was
on flexibility, and this pressed steel machine of
vaguely nautical lines would putt-putt-putt along at
five miles an hour in top gear.

Meanwhile I'd sold the little Mathis. This, again,
was the result of living near the Hog's Back. The long
straight road, entirely empty of all traffic, was an open
invitation to speed, and the dainty progress of the
Mathis at an elegant 38 mph, and less where the
ground sloped upwards, became frustrating.

I went to the Motor Show, and there, on the
Salmson stand, was a pure white two-seater sports
with a boat-shaped tail and black upholstery, marked
'A mile a minute guaranteed'.

In those days beyond recall there were distinctly
gentlemanly salesmen on all the stands with R.F.C.
moustaches and pin-striped suits who would approach
and say, 'Good *morning*, sir! Rather a snappy
little outfit, what? Would you care to try the driving
seat?'

So you got in and found everything fell neatly to
hand, and the desire for ownership stole over you.

'Will she really do sixty?'

'Absolutely guaranteed, sir. In writing. Would you
care to view the machinery?'

He opened the bonnet. The French were neat
mechanics. A machined overhead valve cover. All the

wiring neatly clipped in parallel lines. The starter-
motor and the dynamo highly polished.

'How do you manage to get the speed out of a ten-
horse engine?'

'Very high compression, sir. Overhead valves. High
power-weight ratio. She's nice, isn't she?'

She was very nice.

I mentioned the little matter of a Mathis. He
allowed me a hundred. Money passed. A neat little
card with the word 'SOLD' was hung on the mascot.
Naked lady. And every day while the show lasted, and
without letting the salesman see me, I goggled at that
car.

She did her sixty all right. First time out. The engine
had a terrific kick. The air rushed past. The naked
lady sped before her up the long ribbon of road. I burst
into song. 'Whispering.' 'Dah da-da dah-da dada
DAH DAH....'

The Salmson and I became firm friends, though it
was never a love affair. The car had staggered seating,
which was rather amusing. The passenger sat about
six inches farther from the screen than the driver,
which gave her a lot more wind to cope with and kept
her out of the way. Though I was working at home I
drove to London quite a lot. On principle, really. If
you want to be an author a bit more realistic than
Thomas Hardy or Jane Austen, you must not sit for
seven days a week gazing either at a blank piece of
paper, or Cuttmill pond. You have to get about a bit,
and there was a very friendly A.A. man at the entrance
to Cobham who learned to recognize my face, and
roared with laughter at every one of my changes of car.
What happened to him, I wonder? The Cobham police
had the reputation of being rather hot on the job. That
stretch of road known as 'The Fairmile' was ideal for

stopping any motorist who could be clocked as doing more than 20 mph, and that chap was a very wise prophet if you proposed to cover the territory at a steady 60 mph.

Ah well, all things come to an end. There was a terribly cold winter, and I had become rather keen on going to dances. It was the same old problem, repeated, of the A.V. Monocar. If you wanted to drive a girl somewhere in evening dress, you really couldn't put her six inches behind you in an open car doing a mile a minute.

So, keeping filial step with my mother, and after a visit to Paris where all those pretty little coupés were popping about, I traded the Salmson for a 5cv Citroën coupé.

It was a disaster. It was pretty enough in all conscience, but the feel of the thing was cool iron. The starter made a noise like someone kicking a dustbin. The engine fired like four sledge-hammers. The iron pistons set up a fantastic vibration-period at exactly 20 mph, so that through towns and villages one was limited to 15. There was another shocker at 5 mph either side of 35, and you could really only get through this one by driving at the car's maximum speed, which was about 38.

I'm afraid the Cobham A.A. man was due for a good laugh. The thing was that my mother was also freezing to death in her beastly Citroën, and a man in Guildford, a Mr Crow, talked her into buying a thing called a Triumph Fourteen.

This was a particularly ugly conveyance, with a bonnet which sloped up to the windscreen, and a most offensive rear quarter, which stuck up like a ramrod to meet a flat roof. But it was obviously well made. It had a worm drive in the back axle, low gears, a willing

23

engine, and it climbed the slope up past the hospital to
the Hog's Back in top gear at a positively sporting
rate of knots, and with a healthy burble from the
exhaust.

I was distinctly taken with it, and discovered in
conversation with Mr Crow that they made a Triumph
Ten. As luck would have it there was one in his showrooms. It was positively good-looking, with a splendid
radiator with a hemisphere of the world at the top,
good straight horizontal lines, the coupé part in the
right place, and a fascinating tail which curved round
in the shape of a duck's arse, unlike any car made
before or since.

The moment you got in you could feel and see that
it, too, was beautifully made. The right-hand gear-
change gleamed with plate. The carpets were thick.
There was quite an array of instruments. There was a
leathery smell of leather. Indeed the only thing I could
find against it in the showrooms were the Sankey steel
wheels, which were enough to make any car into a bit
of a gun-carriage.

Well, I bought it, but I never really established an
emotional rapport with it. It was so terribly British. It
was sturdy. It was full of honest workmanship. It was
unimaginative. It was conservative to the point of
absurdity. The engine, you felt, would run for years,
but only at a gentlemanly 'fast saunter'. The gear-
change, through a visible gate, demanded a pause for
reflection and a silent belch between each change of its
nicely matched cogs. It was like a country gentleman,
too full of pork, placing his pipestem between nicely
matched teeth. It wasn't me, but I drove it all the way
to the South of France.

My parents had become Riviera regulars by this
time. They went down on the Blue Train, and a friend

of mine called Michael Trappes-Lomax and I got into
the Triumph, and proceeded without incident to
Newhaven, where they hoisted the car on board by
chains, which did quite a bit of damage to the new
paint. At Dieppe, some hours later, the car was
hoisted ashore in the same way, a couple of stout
planks passed underneath to join chains. Infuriating.
However, we mounted, if that's the word. Michael
was wearing a cloth cap and plus fours. I had my
'*véritable beret basque*', bought on a previous occasion. We set forth among the tramlines and the
stone setts.

The Triumph registered outrage. It didn't like the
tramlines, and it was disgusted by the setts. It rocked
and rattled, angrily. We passed a flock of cyclists
silently, in the traditional British manner. They
shouted, '*Averte !*' They actually wanted horn-
blowing. We had a klaxon. It went grrr. Grr-*ouch*.
A-*Hoo*. A-*Hoo*-er! The Triumph thought this was very
vulgar.

A few years later it became fashionable to go rushing
across France in an effort to beat the Blue Train. The
Blue Train took approximately twenty-four hours. It's
a long way. It's a hell of a long way.

That night we tottered into Chartres, very tired,
and staggered into bed. The next night, after bucking
along frightful roads hour after hour from dawn till
dusk, we slid into Saumur, where the Hôtel de la
Poste had a reputation for putting the ex-chef of the
ex-Kaiser to cook in the kitchen. But we were much too
tired to eat a meal, and fell straight into bed to listen
for the next ten hours to the sound of gigantic lorries
thundering past and the scream of people beating the
Blue Train to Monte Carlo.

By this time, the Triumph, as British as ever and

with absolutely nothing the matter with it, was looking
as raddled as a middle-class matron who had spent two
nights in the ditch. It was covered in alternate layers
of mud and dust, and one of the tyres had a nasty-
looking gash in the sidewall where we must have run
over a bottle. But it held its air. So in the morning,
silently cursing the machine for its stubbornness and
mulish good workmanship, we set out with heavy
hearts. Lyons is a dreadful provincial city of far too
many inhabitants, far too many bridges, no signposts,
and far too many streets all looking exactly the same.
We got abominably lost for about an hour and a half,
but in the end we broke loose and, that night, we made
Avignon.

In the shadow of the Popes we stumbled on a very
modern hotel where they actually knew how to construct a cocktail. Emboldened by this discovery we ate
a magnificent meal. The night air was encouraging too.
There was the smell of mimosa and mock oranges to
blend with the *coq au vin* and the *crustaces Provençales*.

They only had one room, but it had two beds in it
and an attendant bathroom, and we laid ourselves
thankfully to rest. We seemed to be arriving. Unfortunately the dividing walls of the bedrooms were
paper-thin, and we had hardly closed our eyes when
we became aware, with shocking clarity, of a middle-
aged and, doubtless, moustachioed gentleman of
commerce indulging in love-games with his mistress.
The grunts, the trills of laughter, the slappings, the
endearments, the squeals of merriment, even the
kisses—m-m-m—might have been in the very room.
At about half past one we gave him a shout in rehearsed
unison.

'Oh for God's sake SHUT UP!'

26   That did it. I hope the Popes were pleased.

The next morning we took the high road for Monte Carlo. On some high moor one of the tyres sighed sibilantly and went flat.

It wasn't the fault of the car, of course. It was what the French call one of the *desagréments de la route*, but in our exhausted state it seemed like the last straw. We sat in silence. Some larks sang.

We climbed out, and strewed the surrounding heather with our suitcases, pumps, jacks, wheelbraces and all the grisly paraphernalia of a wheel change.

A splendid Rolls-Royce hove quietly into sight beside us, and its chauffeur, looking down on us from a great height, said to whichever of us preferred to be the spokesman, 'Are you all right, sir?'

We told him we had a puncture. He could see that. He made no move to get out but continued to gaze down upon us.

'When I saw the GB I thought I'd better stop.'

'That's very kind of you,' we said.

He sat on. The sun was warm, and we sweated in our heavy plus-four suits.

'I've done a hundred miles this morning.'

'Have you really! We've done about twenty-four.'

'All depends where you start from, doesn't it. I generally like to get in a hundred and fifty before lunch. Then you can take it quietly after. Suppose I'm lucky, really. Not having anybody in the car. You want to hang the wheel from the top stud, mister. Then the others will fall into place. My people don't travel down in the car. They go down in the train. Can't blame them really, I suppose.'

Michael and I swore under our breath.

'Nice little car you've got there.'

'Yes, isn't it.'

'What'll she do?'

'Oh—about fifty, fifty-five.'

The dud wheel was filthy. So were our hands, and the fronts of our suits. We dropped it into the well in the running-board.

'Well—who wants to go fast?'

'Quite.'

We stowed the jack and the tools and began re-assembling the suitcases. If only this ghastly man would go away.

'I generally keep her to not more than seventy myself.'

'Very sensible. And, er, thanks for the good advice.'

'I thought I'd better stop when I saw the GB.'

We got in, one each side, and pulled out the starter. The Rolls didn't move.

'Bloody awful m-m-man,' said Michael, who had a stutter. 'I think he wants us to go first.'

'We can't go first, he'll want us to do fifty-five all the time.'

The Rolls didn't move.

'Oh all right, then!'

We pulled out into the middle of the road and set off through those well-cut gears. The Rolls followed discreetly.

'I can't stand this. Wave him on!'

'Perhaps he just wants to see the wheel doesn't come off.'

'It won't come off. Wave him on!'

We both waved. One each side.

The thing hissed past. The chauffeur touched his cap. We were on our own again. That night, as the sun went behind the *tête du chien* we shambled down the hill into Monte Carlo.

The man at the reception desk, taking stock of our appearance, was sympathetic, almost chiding. The drama of the occasion was heightened by the arrival of my mother and father, looking very clean and rested, in evening dress.

'Good Heavens!' they said. 'What happened to you? Didn't you have a decent journey?'

Michael was polite.

I said we'd had the most horrible journey. We had to fight every inch of the way.

'It is very disagreeable,' said the man behind the desk. 'It should never be attempted. There is a boat for all that.'

'A boat?'

'*Mais bien sûr*. A boat. Once a week. The car goes on the boat. The passengers travel on the *train bleu*. There is a boat for *Angleterre* tomorrow.'

We looked at each other.

'You wish me to arrange?'

We wished him to arrange. I never saw that Triumph again.

CHAPTER II

Early Loves and Marriage

IF WE WANTED to make trips to San Remo or the Gorges du Loup we had to hire cars. We must now be round about the 1925 mark, but all the hire cars in Monaco were unarguably pre-war.

We started with a clumsy old Rochet-Schneider, a big four-cylinder of fantastic stroke-bore ratio which pinked its way up to the Corniche like a steel band. Its driver was very proud of it. '*Complètement remise à neuf*,' he repeated as a sort of refrain to the Anvil Chorus. But the next day I discovered an ancient but honourable Rolls.

I suppose it must have been a Silver Ghost of the 31

sort that, when you opened the bonnet, you appeared
to see two three-cylinder engines arranged in tandem,
one behind the other.

This was the first time I had travelled in a Rolls-
Royce, and I was eager to see how it compared with
our old Daimler Forty-Five.

We set off past the tea-shop called 'A Window in
Thrums'. You could have knocked me down with a
feather. The engine could actually be heard! Quite
loudly, too. You could hear the clutch shaft going
round and round, the valves were popping up and
down, and the gearing was so high that the individual
power impulses banged lustily through the silencer
system. Compared with the Daimler, which in those
days aspired to be the rival of the Rolls, this was
definitely noisy.

What one couldn't hear, of course, was the painstaking workmanship which made the Rolls practically
immortal, so that the speedometer would pass the
99,000 mark time after time, while all the Daimlers
had stopped turning in their graves.

This car could be started overnight by wiggling the
ignition control. I think that, like the Model T Ford,
it had a buzz-box in its circuit which produced sparks
when the magneto wasn't turning. It was a splendid
and impressive trick. All you had to do was to switch
off at night with the mixture control over to 'Rich'.
The pistons were so gas-tight in their cylinders that,
twelve hours later, a spark would find one piston on
compression and ready for firing, and before you could
say 'the Hon. Charlie Rolls' the engine was running.

Thirty years later, when I graduated to the Rolls
class myself, I used to stagger my friends by per-
forming this fantasy on a car which was already twenty
years old.

Monte Carlo is a good place for motorcars. The Voisin was popular, and very pretty when it sported mahogany planking with copper studs, just like the boats in the Condamine. It had a four-cylinder sleeve-valve engine, and the gear-box was there to be used. The Minervas were already extremely impressive with their immensely long bonnets and imperious air.

I was sitting, one day, on a bench in the Casino gardens. The sun shone. The flowers bloomed. The sound of Russian music filtered from the Café de Paris. And sitting at the other end of the same bench was Sir Basil Zaharoff. He was known as 'the mystery man of Europe'. It was said that he actually caused small wars in order to sell the armaments he manufactured to both sides.

I saw a Minerva drive up. It was very elegant indeed, with a taut little *coupé de ville* right at the back, and a very handsome chauffeur sitting out in the open with a chin-strap under his chin.

The back door opened. A man descended, walked up to the chauffeur, and struck him across the face with a pair of gloves. The chauffeur remained impassive. I could see, out of the corner of my eye, that the mystery man of Europe was watching the scene.

'That man', I said, 'must be a German.'

'That man', Sir Basil echoed my words, 'is my brother.'

I left the bench rather hurriedly, wondering whether the length of a bonnet and the six-cylinder sleeve inside could alter the character of a man. I am pretty sure that the Mercedes driver, in all countries, British as well as black, does acquire a touch of the Teutonic.

The Belgian Minerva reminds me that somebody had parked a Spyker immediately outside the hotel. This was a very rare beast. It had the most fascinating

33

wheels, and the hub caps had beautifully made and
very visible serrations fitting precisely into the splines
of the axle. It looked like the product of a watch-
maker.

Ah, *nostalgie*! In those twenties the French cars,
apart from the Voisin, were still a bit embryonic. The
Delage showed no sign that it would blossom one day
into the most beautiful artifact ever produced by man.
Even the Hispano-Suiza, with its shapely Guynemayer
stork and its pencil-thin radiator, was still in its Alfonso
stage. The elephant-trunked Renaults were frightful,
but not so frightful as the Mercedes of the period, a
monument to German ugliness and brutality, with its
sharply pointed snout and a hideous, pterodactylian
appendage at the rear for concealing, with painted tin,
the existence of a hood.

I went home and bought another Amilcar. Which
reminds me of Dr Johnson, who said, 'Fools build
houses and wise men live in 'em.' The same applies to
motorcars. All the cars I have lost my heart to, except
one, have been second-hand. The reason is absurdly
simple. For the same amount of money you get a
much better car. Its condition, within limits, is im-
material. Any piece of machinery can be put in order
and made to work. And any new car, once driven out
of the showroom on its own number plates, sheds its
purchase tax and one third of its initial value.

I said, 'except one'. There used to be a chap on the
far side of Hammersmith Bridge called Vernon Balls,
who specialized in Amilcars. And the moment I saw
this adorable little Weymann saloon I knew I had to
have it. It had a high waistline, helmet wings, steps
instead of running boards, and the whole line of the
thing was impeccable, except at the back, where a
deliberately false angle had been suggested rather than

introduced, as if to cock a snook or flounce a skirt at all the cars one passed.

So I bought it, new. Fortunately my first two novels had been quite absurdly successful and I had the money in my pocket. I never could resist a pretty shape, and this one was covered in a shiny blue-grey material with an alligator pattern stamped into it.

The inside of those Weymann bodies was always luxurious. By some magic this little motorcar had been given two sofas on which four men could loll, and all the little fittings like side-lamps and ash trays were square, and original, and seemed cut like jewels.

I drove it down to Guildford in triumph. The Amilcar's little engine sang. It was as different from the Triumph as Chanel No. 5 from Stilton cheese. But it was a very little engine. When I got past the station and began the long haul up to the Hog's Back, we went screaming up in second gear. I could see my mother's Triumph wuffling up in top to disappear into the *ewigkeit*.

That was the only place where I became a little red-faced, that climb to the Hog's Back. It would go *down* the hill at a beautifully controlled sixty. It would drive to London at any speed you liked, up hill and down dale, never putting a foot wrong. But come slowly round the entrance to Guildford station, and did that gear-box shriek!

It was while I was running this car that the General Strike broke out. My father felt he had to cover the scene from the dedicated journalist's point of view, and as I also felt constrained to do my bit in the class war I offered to ferry him to London and back every day.

It really was a class war, and very dangerous at that. The social side of it was emphasized by the rush of the so-called upper and middle classes to 'volunteer'. Just

as they did in the early years of the war. It became a
noble duty. And they dressed for the part. They drove
giant locomotives in bowler hats and spats. They conducted buses in plus fours and lemon-yellow gloves.
They hung rolled umbrellas on the drivers' doorways
of tube trains. The girls delivered the milk. Churchill
started a newspaper. In villages all over England the
letters were delivered on horseback. And Hammersmith Broadway became a very perilous place.

They threw stones at the buses and the windscreens of young gentlemen preening themselves in
all-aluminium Vauxhall Thirty-Ninety-eights, and
offering lifts to commuters as they came out of the
station. The people scowled and shouted. It was
definitely ugly. On the fourth day we watched a
General Omnibus stopped by the mere press of angry
men and then slowly tilted till it overturned with an
almighty crash of glass. For the first time since
Cromwell, English blood ran in the gutters, but thank
God no one was killed.

One more day, just one more day of this, and out-
right, killing war seemed inevitable. I persuaded my
father to damp his ardour and let us get the hell out. I
set the Amilcar scudding across Hammersmith Bridge
till we were stopped by a young Frenchman with a
briefcase and an anxious face. He wanted to go to
Wimbledon. We didn't want to go to Wimbledon, but
we did want to go up Putney High Street to hit the
Portsmouth Road, so we told him to hop in.

We opened the door for him at the top of the hill
and pointed out Wimbledon Common. He was furious.

'Wimbledon!' he shouted, catching the prevailing
anger.

'Putney,' we said gently.

36   The next day Sir John Simon arose in the House of

Commons and announced that the General Strike was illegal. Without a day's hesitation all the strikers except the miners returned to work. The British are a very remarkable people.

Now, about a year after these vivid events, something happened to me which radically altered my life. I decided that I wanted to get married. Or perhaps it was the lady I decided I wanted to marry who decided that. I've never been absolutely certain. At all events the question of money became suddenly of overriding importance.

Living at home and writing novels and short stories meant that all the money I earned was there to be spent. I could buy Amilcars at will. I had my eye on the Straight Eight. But the awful responsibility of providing a house, and food, and furniture, coupled with our decision to live in London, obviously meant that we had to do without a motorcar at all. I had to abandon one love for the sake of the other. So the Amilcar was sold.

My mother and father, considerably shaken by my decision to start life on my own, suddenly came to the conclusion that they couldn't continue to live in the country, and that they had better move back to London too, so as to be near us. In no time at all the house was sold, and the Triumph with it, and they settled down near Sloane Square, where my mother solaced herself with a brand-new black Weymann Willys-Knight with scarlet wheels.

If the truth must be told, and where cars are concerned it always must, the Willys-Knight engine knocked spots off the similar design installed in the Daimler. It appeared that it was not inevitable that the sleeve-valve engine was given to endemic vibration at speeds above 50 mph. The Willys was not only

inaudible, it could not be felt either; and in uncanny
silence and smoothness it produced rocket acceleration
which pinioned everybody in their seats until the foot
was lifted. It induced, I should guess, from subsequent experience in the air, something in the region
of 3g, and the only car I have driven which came anywhere near it was the SK supercharged Mercedes.
But more of that one later.

Without my Amilcar, and still unmarried, I borrowed the Willys constantly, and drove my fiancée
down to Peaslake, where we now live. We used to cross
the Downs to Shere to avoid the 'out by Dorking and
back by Guildford' round which in those days exer-
cised a mesmeric effect on the pleasure motorist. On
every fine afternoon they streamed along, in solemn
procession, all doing exactly thirty. The middle-class
motoring scene was now largely dominated by the
Austin Twenty and the Armstrong-Siddeley Fourteen,
but of course there was a far, far greater choice than
there is today. Alberts, Calcotts, Calthorpes, Swifts,
Morgans, Hudsons, Essexes, Humbers, Palladians,
Beans, Tamplins, Delahayes, Talbots, Sunbeams,
Delages, Buicks, Fords, Cardens, O.M.s, Fiats,
Roamers, Rovers, Lanchesters, those *hideous* early
Lagondas, A.C.s, Gregoire-Campbells, Salmsons,
E.N.V.s . . . : the variety was unending, and they all
went out by Dorking and back by Newlands Corner
and Guildford, so that if you were trying to cross the
stream at Shere you had an enforced Motor Show.

The Willys-Knight, with its leathercloth body, its
wooden wheels and its 4½-litre six-cylinder sleeve-
valve engine, had the heels of all of them. It looked
quite decent, too, with its pleasantly proportioned four-
window, blank-rear-quarter shape, and a really resplendent chromium-plated knight thrusting a lance

38

atop a radiator whose lines were subsequently imitated to the point of slavery by the entire Buick range.

Then something happened. I won't tell you what it was, but there was a hitch. The marriage was off. And the parents, reacting with almost unnecessary violence, closed the house, sold the car and took a house in Cobham, with some idea that if I was isolated there, carless, I should live to get over my disappointment. So I bought a 14/40 Vauxhall.

I drove that car, daily, along the new Kingston By-pass. Fortunately it was summer, and the car ran with an agreeably floating motion in the sunshine. It was as British as the Triumph Ten but very smooth and long-legged. It had a nice high radiator and bonnet with the famous Vauxhall flutes, and the short back and sides tucked neatly behind the instrument board. It was a great pity that this was the last of the true Vauxhalls before they had to sell to General Motors. They were good cars, and the Thirty-Ninety-eight, of course, was, and still is, one of the great ones.

Then, with unnatural suddenness, the hitch was overcome, and the marriage was on again. Once again good intentions came into play. I had to sell the Vauxhall and put the money towards the last two years of a ninety-nine-year lease of a charming little house in Cheltenham Terrace, which is just off the King's Road in Chelsea, with the open parade-ground of the Duke of York's in front and the grass and trees of Burton Court just at the bottom. I got married all right, but before we moved in we went for a honeymoon to Nice, where an uncle of mine had an empty flat which he had taken to establish French residence in order to get a divorce.

While we were down there we happened to pass the Mathis showrooms, where they had a six-cylinder 39

sedan standing in the window with the words À
LOUER scrawled on a card.

This seemed like an awfully good idea, so we went
in and began the negotiations. This involved filling in
an unending form.

'Place of birth, M'sieur?'

'Nationality of parents, M'sieur?'

'Carte d'identité numéro?'

I produced British passports. 'We, George Nathan-
ial Curzon—'

'Ah oui. Driving licence, M'sieur?'

I dived into the back pocket of my trousers and
came up with my British licence.

His eyes filled with tears as he handed it back.

'I regret, M'sieur. Je regrette infiniment.' He began
to tidy the papers, as though the episode were closed.

'Je regrette, mais celle-ci est inutilizable.'

'Inuti—' I couldn't say it. 'Why not? I've driven all
over France with that.'

'In your own car? To hire a car in France the rule is
different. It is necessary to have a French driving
licence.'

'Oh my goodness me! Well, can't I get one?'

Sudden hope sprang in his eyes.

'Ah! I give you a note to the Juge d'Instruction. First
you pay a deposit, no?'

The forms came out again, and he scratched away
with a lot of French sevens. Money passed. And he
drew a map. To the end of the Avenue Victor Hugo.
Right, across the railway line. Left at the gaz. In a
field we would find the Juge d'Instruction. Could I
remember the title? 'Juge d'Instruction'.

The car was wheeled across the pavement on a
couple of planks. Petrol was poured in. It was a black
sedan, square-cut, with a high pointed prow. The

40

engine started quietly. One of those dynamotors by
the sound of it. Off we went, to the end of the Avenue
Victor Hugo, right, over the railway line, and there
was the big gasometer, with a field in front of it and an
iron gate with a notice:

'PERMIT DE CONDUIRE.

PRIÈRE D'ENTRER.'

We entered. There was a little man with puffed
cheeks and a puffable moustache, looking exactly like
Hercule Poirot. He gestured us to a halt in the road.

'*Monsieur le Juge d'Instruction?*'

He blew himself up and nodded.

I handed him the note. He read it, nodded, and
pointed to a place inside the iron fence, where,
presumably, we were to stand and wait.

So we got out and sat on the top of the railings,
dressed all in white and looking frightfully British.

There was a sort of cinder track cut in the field, and
round this a number of enormously fat Frenchmen
were circling, hunched over minute mopeds. The noise
of tiny engines buzzing at full throttle rose like a
scream, and, from a raised platform, *Monsieur le
Juge* conducted them, like the ring master at a circus.
Round and round they went, heads down into the
wind, jowls and moustachios flapping, tiny front wheels
jumping and wobbling.

I'm afraid we laughed. In our superior white linen,
we laughed, and stopped suddenly. *Monsieur le Juge*
flung us a scowl that would have stopped an orchestra.
We eyed each other into shame-faced silence.

After about a quarter of an hour he began to flag
down riders as they passed. They couldn't stop, but
after a series of terrifying swerves they made a final
circuit, dismounted and came over, still bent double
over their ridiculous machines. A little ceremony

took place. Papers changed hands. There was a handshake.

When the lot of them had been passed *Monsieur le
Juge* got down from his rostrum, pulled a key out of
his pocket, locked the iron gate with a clang, and got
into the front passenger seat of our car.

'*Allez!*' he said.

We swarmed in after him, reversed neatly, and approached the end of the Avenue Victor Hugo.

'*À gauche!*'

We drove back into Nice, past the flat, past the
Albert Premier gardens, to that old part of the town
where there are arcades and shops in a jumble of dis-
order.

'*À droit! À gauche! Encore à gauche! Stop!*'

We were in front of a greengrocer.

Monsieur le Juge, blowing up his moustache, let
himself out of the door. He approached the shop
where a cornucopia of fruit and vegetables spilled over
the pavement. He selected a nice melon, a couple of
cauliflowers and a bag of oranges. He placed all this
on the back seat with an apology to Madame and
climbed back in beside me.

'*Allez!*'

We drove him to a *charcuterie*, a *marchand de vin*,
and a *boucherie*. The back seat was now piled high with
strong-smelling cheeses, and a whole sliding assort-
ment of edibles including a large ham and a rather
drippy parcel of pigs' trotters.

I must say I rather enjoyed all this. It was pleasant
to be at the wheel of a car again and to show a neat
avoidance of bicycles, pedestrians, scavenging dogs
and the other hazards of back-street Nice. My heart
rather warmed to the little man. He was showing us
42 life. I was showing him how a car ought to be driven.

Finally, after about half-an-hour's shopping we set forth once more.

'*Allez! Tout droit. Tout droit. Tout droit. Ça-y-est. Stop!*'

We were outside a block of flats. He began staggering to collect his provender. Gallantly we came to his rescue, struggling with the ham and the cheeses and the bottles and dumping them in an empty lift. When all was transported I held out my hand, feeling really quite friendly, for the handshake and the licence.

'*Vous n'avez pas passé*,' he said.

I could see from his face that he could see from my face that the intelligence had not registered.

So he repeated, '*Vous n'avez pas passé!*'

And he went up in the lift.

This time the Mathis man really wept, great salt tears. We described our experience. Sorrowfully he unlocked the drawer to return our money. Then a thought struck him.

'Did you pay him a thousand francs?'

'*A thousand francs?*'

'*Mais, naturellement.* For his trouble.'

'Good Lord, no! It never entered my head.'

He stopped unlocking the drawer and held out his hand. I placed a thousand francs there.

'I will arrange everything. It is the custom, you understand. The custom of the country.'

Next morning, the Mathis was standing outside our door.

I won't go on about that Mathis, though it did have one extraordinary feature. When you opened that spectacular bonnet there was nothing, literally nothing, inside it. The top of the engine was level with the chassis. That, no doubt, was why it crawled smoothly up the Corniche, and silked along the Promenade des

43

Anglais, and refused, like a reluctant show-jumper,
if you put it at anything steeper than about one in
eight. But, as I say, enough of the honeymoon Mathis.
The time has come to talk of Austin Sevens.

CHAPTER III

Foreign Affairs

THE ORIGINAL Austin Seven Chummy was, to my
way of thinking, rather an unattractive little car. And
it certainly wasn't the first really small conventional
car, as many people seem to think. There had been a
Humber Voiturette years before, and France was
crawling with baby Peugeots.

Its great disadvantage was a whippy crankshaft
with one bearing at either end. Is it possible that one
of these was a roller? Anyway, the net result was that
it rattled around, making horrid noises and setting
up a sympathetic vibration in the starting handle, so
that you travelled along ringing like an electric bell. 45

The only possible way to quieten that crankshaft was
to retard the ignition. This did the trick, but it made
the exhaust rather noisy and limited the maximum
speed to about thirty-seven.

The body, of course, was very elementary. It had a
sort of cock-up at the back, and when the hood was
raised the ironwork was brutally apparent. And its
horn mooed like a cow. Except that any sort of car is
better than no sort of car, I, personally, would not
have been seen in one, until the coming of the
Swallow.

Mr Lyons, as he then was, had been making some
distinctly snappy sidecars for attachment to motorcycles. He obviously had an eye for line. And when the
Austin Swallow suddenly burst upon my conscious-
ness I obtained a catalogue and brooded on it, lustfully,
in bed.

'Cream and Crimson', it said.

My wife was expecting a baby in about four months'
time. This meant that she was largely immobilized.
She was a little worried about the whole business of
making a *new* life, and I told myself she needed something violently extroverted to make her snap out of it.
What was needed, I thought, was a *fait accompli*.

'Cream and Crimson'.

Mr Lyons had certainly done a job on the Austin
Seven. A svelte, fairly fastback saloon sitting well
down behind the engine compartment, with an over-
bold radiator topped by a swallow up in front. There
was a beaded waistline in the right place, and the thing
gleamed with wet cream below, and wet crimson
above.

I'm afraid I fell. I not only ordered one, to be delivered in two weeks' time, but I also fixed up with the
R.A.C. to get all the *carnets* and things to take the car

to France, and booked rooms at her favourite place called the Abbaye, at St-Jacut-de-la-Mer, in Brittany.

Some *fait accompli!*

There are really only two ways to take a car to Brittany. One is to travel on the night boat to St Malo, in which case you miss a night's sleep; the other is to cross in the daytime to Dieppe and drive the 200 miles before supper. I hate doing without sleep, so we drove down to Newhaven.

The seats were very low, so that we couldn't see much. There was no silencer, and the open exhaust bellowed like Chitty Chitty Bang Bang. The starting handle was ringing heavily away in front, and the suitcases on the rudimentary back seat bounced like a bad horsewoman, and kept hitting us in the neck.

Fortunately the sea was like glass. We ate a meal and snoozed in deck chairs with the sun on our faces.

When the car was craned ashore, the effect on the little French crowd would have gratified a prima donna. They had never seen anything like it. They oohed and ahhed.

'*Trés practique*', they said, '*pour deux ou trois personnes.*'

But there was one of those beastly little French boys, with short pants and socks and an expression of malign intelligence.

'*Cyclistes Americaines!*' he shouted.

Then he saw the swallow. He came up and stuck a sallow face in the window as we were getting in.

'*Oiseau de mauvais augur!*' he hissed.

We gave him a blast of the exhaust, and bucked about over the tramlines and stone setts. A door handle fell in the road. I hadn't the moral courage to retrieve it. It was then that we made our final discovery. The car was entirely without springs.

47

I must say, my wife was marvellous.

For 200 miles we banged and crashed from pothole to pothole, mooing like a cow, with the exhaust roaring, the whole car obviously disintegrating beneath us. Somewhere just before Mont St Michel the back of the exhaust came free and began rutting and scraping behind us. At Dinan the whole thing fell on to the road with a loud musical clang, which was a great relief. We left it where it was. At this point some pretty lethal exhaust fumes began to enter the car, but we had only ten miles to go, and by hanging our heads out of the windows we managed to survive—the three of us.

The Abbaye is run as a sort of guest house by a gaggle of nuns, and for anybody with a philosophy which takes no account of the filthiest lavatories in all the great country of France, it makes a pleasant spot for a holiday. There are marvellous coves and beaches all round a little peninsula and an island about a mile offshore to which one can sail when the tide is high, and walk when it is low.

I found a splendid old mechanic down a pit beneath a great deal of broken machinery who was a masterly improviser. He wore a beret and a blue blouse, and a dead Caporal hung permanently from his lower lip. No nonsense about 'obtaining replacement parts'! He produced a length of rusty iron pipe, filled it with sand, bent it, hammered it, spat on it, welded it, and came up with an exhaust pipe *and* a silencer. It was he who gave me the tip about retarding the ignition to stop that crankshaft whipping. Those two things alone made a surprising difference. But he also brought out a handful of Solex main jets from his pocket. Every evening at six when the sun began to cool I used to screw one of these things in and go for a short run around the countryside to try the effect. A very slight enrichment of the mixture did slow the explosion, so that we were able to give the ignition a shade more advance. At the end of a week we had an entirely different car, which was even occasionally capable of spring movement. I have no idea how he achieved this, but I suspect he jettisoned one or two of the leaves and threw away the Hartfords.

I had been promised a bath by Thursday. With casual innocence I had demanded this after the first day or two, not imagining the complexity of the arrangement.

Two little nuns inclined their heads solemnly.

'It will be ready by Thursday, *M'sieur*.'

I had noticed a small, pagoda-like building in the centre of the main courtyard. After some time smoke began to arise from this. At all hours of the day and night two fluttering little figures could be discerned hurrying guiltily in with baskets of charcoal. And the people, sitting in deck-chairs, watched the movement with interest.

'Somebody must have ordered a bath!' they said.

I was attacked by an Englishman.

'What d'you want to have a *bath* for? Can't you bathe in the sea?'

I said I wanted to wash off all the young oysters and seaweed.

'Well, I think it's disgusting,' he said.

I think my wife would have liked to stay on at St Jacut until our time was up, but I revolted at the lavatories. They were quite nice lavatories really, with large cisterns and heavy iron chains. Their only fault was that the good nuns had neglected to connect up a water supply, so that the corridors in the mornings resounded to the rattle of chains and the hollow clank of empty enamelware.

Our original plan had been to spend a couple of days at the Abbaye, and then make our way south through the Landes country to St-Jean-de-Luz, of which we had good reports.

I feel penitent about it now, but I made rather a point about moving on. On the Thursday, my wife listened to the new quietness of the Swallow, and rather reluctantly gave in.

I grabbed our thin suitcases, flung an absurdly small number of francs to the nuns, and off we went. I always wonder who had that bath.

It was a great improvement. And the roads we encountered were rippled minor roads rather than the potholed *Routes Nationales* of the previous day. With the new softness of our suspension the Swallow wallowed comfortably, and at the end of the first hour my wife announced that she wanted to be sick.

This was appalling. And this time there was no argument. We lurched on to a place called Carnac, saw a sign-board reading CARNAC PLAGE. We looked at each other. Obviously this was to be our St-Jean-de-Luz. I pushed the Swallow's nose up the turning, and presently we espied an attractive little hotel called, appropriately I thought, Les Genets, which means 'the Plantagenista', from which the Plantagenets took their name.

As we went in we were assailed by a powerful smell. It was duck roasting.

This boded pretty well. A cheerful, talkative lady had rooms. They were spotlessly clean, and the lavatories were superb. It was still out of season, the lady explained, and the only visitors were the proprietors of other hotels and restaurants, on hand to make ready for when the customers would arrive.

I had noticed two or three of those small black
Renaults parked before the doors. Square, heavily built, sound and comfortable-looking men were all around with napkins tucked in their waistcoats.

The first dish was a great bowl of unidentifiable shell fish. They were in movement. I stared. One of them opened its shell, protruded a short length of tube, went 'F-F-F' and shut up.

I stared with fascination and horror. They were all doing it.

'F-F-F'

'F-F-F'

On every hand was the crackle of shells, the champ of teeth, general guzzle, and that despairing last 'F-F-F' as the wretched things disappeared down gullets to meet the digestive juices. We looked at each other. Impossible.

I ordered a bottle of Moulin-à-Vent.

Quietly we lowered our eyes when the proprietress came to take away a totally untasted dish.

Then came the duck. It was cooked with imagination, sensitivity and a touch of genius. It was golden brown, and it set the juices romping. But there was no duck. There was simply duck skin, with a few shreds adhering to it, a potato, and a green salad on the side.

That night we went to bed, swimming in Moulin-à-Vent but utterly unnourished. For breakfast, of course, there was no breakfast, in the French manner. Half a cup of coffee, a croissant and some apricot jam. At eleven o'clock we had rather a chilly bathe. At the end of it I could have eaten two steaks with a fried egg atop each, a mountain of potatoes and a treacle roll. Not a bit of it. Another bowl of effing bivalves and a peach.

After this, while my wife went up to rest, I went

down to the Swallow, and revved it off in search of
food. Carnac was tight shut. There were a lot of
Dolmens about but not a single shop was open except
for the sale of postcards.

I came across a signpost which read 'Quiberon'. The
arithmetic made it eleven miles. Very well then,
Quiberon.

The way was along an oddly narrow promontory,
with the sea on either side. At that moment Quiberon
was in the news. A young Frenchman, Alain Gerbault,
had sailed around the world single-handed and made
landfall at an island called Belle-Isle. There *must* be
food in Quiberon!

There was. But only a *pâtisserie*. They sold delicious
chocolate éclairs, rich cakes dripping with pink goo,
coconut biscuits, and Gold Flake cigarettes. I bought
a packet of ten, and staggered out to the car, my arms
filled with cream buns. I sat in the car, watching the
waves lapping the sea wall, and wolfed the lot.

It was a good idea about buying only ten cigarettes.
It became a regular feature of Carnac life that I
crawled into the Swallow and popped over to Quiberon
for a packet of cigarettes. My wife, who never had the
slightest interest in food and wasn't particularly
hungry at the moment, thought it was boredom. It
wasn't. It was chocolate éclairs. It can't have been
particularly healthy, but it was a damned sight
healthier than starving to death.

Those little Renaults were all over the place. I rather
liked the look of them. They still had the Renault
snout, with the radiator behind the engine, but the
shape had been refined to quite reasonable proportions. Moreover, they possessed two large and comfortable seats upholstered in wool, a sensible line, a
52 pleasant absence of scarlet paint, and when they

moved they puttered along very flexibly in top gear.
When you knocked them accidentally with your
knuckles *en passant*, the metal seemed immensely thick.
If the opportunity presented itself I had half a mind to
make the change.

The opportunity presented itself almost immediately. Evidently we had written separate postcards to our parents. Evidently we had pitched it far
too strong. I must have said there was no food in the
hotel and that I was fainting from starvation. My wife
must have said she was fainting from being motored
inexorably all over France.

The result was startling. Lady Martin turned up at
the Abbaye in St Jacut and sent telegrams that we must
return there immediately by train. And my father
suddenly arrived in Carnac, his suitcase stuffed with
tins of cocoa and condensed milk.

On consideration this made things very simple.
My wife mounted the train for St Jacut, and I
Swallowed my father to Sloane Square. On arrival I
bought a copy of the Autocar. Yes, there were
Renaults. A chap in Kingston. The next morning I
went down to see him, and came back in a Renault,
second-hand, considerably enriched in the process.

It wasn't until I was the possessor of such a car that I
discovered what made it tick. It had a top gear ratio
of six and a half to one. This formidable oddity was
made necessary by the great weight of metal being
towed by an absurdly small engine of about 700 cc.
When I went down to Kingston again the next day to
complain, I found that the car would ascend Putney
Hill in top gear, but only at 10 mph. When I dropped
down to second gear and made the engine scream, it
would only do 9.

This clearly wouldn't do, and I could not think what 53

had got into the French. I said all this with some
passion when I had puttered up to the garage. The
chap was very nice about it. He said what I wanted was
the Six. He had a Six which was two years older than
the Four and a flat swop would be in order.

This time I asked for a trial run. That chap really
demonstrated very well. We fled round blocks of flats
and in and out of suburban avenues. Clearly the thing
had bags of power, and the engine was silent and
sweet. So that was the car which I drove into Victoria
Station that same afternoon.

My wife said she thought it looked tatty. It did rather.
It wore an elderly Weymann body which some
amateur had decided, not very successfully, to paint a
faded chocolate brown.

So the three of us got in, which we certainly
couldn't have done with the Swallow, and bless my
soul if *that* car didn't have a top gear of six and a half
to one!

I only discovered this a few days later when trying
the thing out for speed along the Kingston By-pass.
At anything above 35 mph that engine was going
round as if it were doing 70. I thought of my Vauxhall,
and the Amilcars and the good old Willys-Knight, and
here I was in a shabby old buzz-box with a beastly
piece of machinery hurling itself round like a dancing
dervish. So I turned down into Kingston and had
further words with the chap.

I cannot think, at this distance, how I allowed
myself to be trapped into this unending series of
Renaults. Actually there were two more. But more of
that anon. This time I think a little money must have
passed, because I emerged, an hour or so later, blinking in the sunlight, at the wheel of an open drophead
of really giant proportions.

Now that was a *good* car. It was old, but with a touch
of faded aristocracy. It had a long bonnet whose front
end was almost out of sight, and it had a nice, big,
lazy, powerful, six-cylinder engine which wafted it
along as effortlessly as you pleased.

There's nothing like a really big car, is there? They
sit down on their springs. They roll. The motion is
lordly. The seat height allows one to look down with
quiet self-possession on the minnows scuttling all
about to get out of the way. This was one of my great
cars.

The trouble was, as we shall learn later, that when-
ever I achieved greatness my wife would say at inter-
vals, 'I can't think how you can afford to run a car like
that. It gives people the wrong ideas. How many miles
does it do to the gallon?'

She did twelve; but I succeeded in keeping her for
well over a year. We never went abroad in it, though it
would have coped magnificently with the undulations,
the potholes and the stone setts. But we went down to
Devonshire once or twice, and when my son was born
we would cram the four of us (the fourth was his
nurse) on to the single seat and waft off for Cambridge,
where my in-laws were thinking of retiring and settling
down.

In those happy days we used to take a house in
Littlehampton for a few months in the summer, and I
actually commuted the 120 miles to London and back
in that grand old lady with no sense of strain whatsoever.

But it's always the same. Every time I get a car I
really like, the business of petrol consumption raises
its head. The Renault did twelve. She was a relic of the
days before high compressions and leaded petrols,
when the only way to get enough power to drive a

motorcar with any sensation of mastery was to have a big engine. It still is, in my opinion, though only the Americans and a few very specialist makes acknowledge it today.

So the old lady went the way of all flesh. I must have gone mad. I swapped her for another of those damned Renault twelve-horsepower Sixes.

I must say the new and last Renault I ever owned looked distinctly snappy. That was the time when Renault themselves made their tremendous gesture, and put the radiator in front of the engine. It was quite a bold, slatted affair, and they had really gone to town with the bodywork. The whole, very solid machine was painted pale primrose yellow, contrasted with thick black mouldings along the waistline and round the windows. The doors continued up to and across the top of those windows, but the whole head was canvas and could be unbuttoned and rolled back. Inside was black patent leather upholstery!

As always with the Renault of that period the thickness of metal was more suitable for a lorry, so of course they had to put in a top gear of $6\frac{1}{2}$:1.

This one didn't vibrate. They must have added an extra bearing or two. All the same one is always uncomfortably aware of an engine whizzing round at about 5000 revs, and the motion of the car was extraordinarily reminiscent of travel by tram. It swanned along quite nicely with a lot of hidden machinery going round somewhere underneath, and if I had put in a bell to stamp on, the illusion would have been complete.

As I say the vehicle looked fetching, and the first time I drove it after taking delivery I had to meet someone at Paddington Station. The policeman saluted and, obviously impressed, said, 'Latest model, Sir?'

Not even that official respect reconciled me to the car. I spent the whole of the next year trying to get rid of it. It wasn't easy. For instance, when my wife disappeared for a weekend with her parents at Cambridge I took the opportunity to pop down to that chap in Kingston and exchange it for another of the big 'uns. When my wife turned up on Monday she shed bitter tears and made me pop down once more and change it back.

I drove it frequently to Cambridge. We went down to Devonshire. We took a summer house, this time in Rustington. It was called Little ffynches, which made me want to sign my name 'Anthony ggibbs'. It was a maddening machine. It never went wrong. It never failed to start. It never even had a puncture. Not a fleck of rust appeared. It climbed all hills in top gear. There was absolutely no excuse to get rid of it whatever.

Then I had the idea of a lifetime. I gave it to my father-in-law, who had smashed up his old bull-nosed Morris. I bought a Daimler.

It was a very old Daimler, a sleeve-valve of course, known in its generation as the Daimler Twenty, and it had a most unusual body by Martin Walter. It was a fixed-head coupé, except that the back half wasn't fixed at all. You climbed in, two steps up, reached up to the roof, undid a couple of those landaulette clamp things, rather like the domestic window latch, climbed down again, 'broke' two hood-irons, and down she creaked.

There were some very pleasing touches here and there. For instance, where the folding part of the roof met the fixed part—I'm speaking of the interior—there was the most enchanting little line of decorated tape, of the type one used to find in first-class carriages of the London, Brighton, and South Coast Railway. Behind the two front seats there was quite a bit of space, and, blow me if the two leather loops didn't unfold two London Taxi seats, facing forwards. What's more, there was a walnut cabinet between them which, on opening, revealed a large hole for a decanter of whisky, and four smaller holes for glasses.

Definitely an equipage. It was painted a rather ugly green, and some former owner had done the top of the bonnet black. I didn't like this, as it introduced my *bête noire*, a rising horizontal line. I soon killed that one by having the top of the boot done black as well, sloping down to, and including, the famous petrol tank slats.

She moved with quite a majestic hiss, and when in motion emitted an astonishing and formidable cloud of bright blue smoke which entirely blotted out all following traffic, giving a marked sense of privacy to the occupants.

Now, two great friends of ours, Conor and Ines Carrigan, came round one day to say they were setting out across France in their brand new Humber Snipe. This was, of course, the Humber Humber Snipe, and no connection with Rootes. And where were they going? Of all places St-Jean-de-Luz!

My wife and I looked at each other. Would it be a splendid atonement for the Austin Swallow if we achieved the journey by Daimler? In unison we asked if it would be in order if we came too?

Ines Carrigan clapped her hands.

It really was absurdly simple. We blotted out the road to Chartres, spent the night, blotted out the road to Paris, spent the night at the Hôtel Napoleon, where they used to fill your lighter at the bar with scented petrol, obliterated the Place de la Concorde from sight on the following morning, and left a majestic and

1906 Argyll
M.M.M.

Above: *1913
4-cylinder Métal-
lurgique*
M.M.M.

Right: *1913 9.5 hp
Model 'S' Standard*
M.M.M.

Left: *1914 9.5 hp Standard*
M.M.M.

Below: *1914 4-cylinder 26 hp Métallurgique*
M.M.M.

1914 20 hp Austin with Grosvenor body
M.M.M.

Above left: *1915
30 hp Austin
Landaulette*
B.M.C.

Above: *1922
Hispano Suiza*
D.T.C.L.

Below left: *1921
8 hp A.V. Monocar*
M.M.M.

Centre right: *The
author's 1924
Martin Walter
6-cylinder sleeve-
valve Daimler 20*

Right: *The author's
1924 1200 cc
Triumph 10*

1924 Isotta
Fraschini Type 8
with Fleetwood
body built for
Rudolph Valentino
M.M.M.

impenetrable vapour-trail all the way down that marvellous Landes country, and arrived, in perfectly good
order; no bumps in the night, no rattles, nothing but
the high whine of the tyres and that bellying cloud of
cerulean blue.

In St-Jean I did a caddish thing. I bought the in-
comparable Guynemayer stork, supposed to grace the
radiator of the Hispano-Suiza, and stuck it atop the
Daimler in place of the Boyce temperature gauge. In
slim flight above the British thumb-marks of the Daimler, it gave the impression of a disapproving dowager
wearing something comic to amuse the children.

Conor and Ines had done it in two days. We didn't
envy them. A Daimler, after all, is different. One lolls.
One enjoys the scenery. But Conor was occasionally
violent. Those were the days when yellow lights were
obligatory in France. The Humber's were white. And
the natives developed an alarming and repugnant
habit of charging full tilt on the wrong side of the
road. His foot went down on the accelerator, and at the
very last second he would swerve violently and shout
'*Allez au diable!*' in very creditable French.

I must tell you something which was absolutely
nothing to do with cars. I had an extremely rich and
expensive dressing gown which my uncle had bought
for me as a present at Harboro's in Bond Street. It was
scarlet, with golden dragons.

After I had been down to the beach once or twice in
this, two girls in a neighbouring tent exclaimed to each
other, '*Ah! Le bel Anglais!*'

Not bad, eh?

And my wife, who had bought a very pretty striped
blue and white summer frock at that little place next
door to the Casino, got her ovation as well.

'*Ah! Comme elle est ravissante!*'

Ah, well—

One day, when I was having a look under the bonnet I discovered rather a neat device I had not spotted before. That bonnet, by the way, does anyone remember? There were two levers like rifle bolts which, when shifted, allowed the central part to rise. The sides then fell apart. Leading into the carburettor was a great copper pipe, with a rotatable collar. I rotated it. Large holes appeared. Obviously a hot or cold air supply.

I banged all the bits together again, and started the engine. The hiss was much louder, but there was one other change of rather disappointing significance—no smoke.

So we Daimlered sedately into Spain, and up the hills to Pau, and, when the fortnight was over, back to Paris, Dieppe and Newhaven to the house in Tite Street.

It was now 1930, a year which I personally regard as the time when the motorcar first reached perfection. It is a very strange thing, that the nostalgists have enraptured themselves with the 'veterans' which run, historically, from the birth of motoring to the First World War, and the 'vintage' machines which end abruptly and arbitrarily at 1930, at the precise moment when the motorcar blossomed in a flowering which it had never attained before and has never regained since.

In performance, in elegance of line, in artistry, in balance, in comfort, in silence and the sheer joy to travel in and behold, the aristocrats with the great names make the years 1930 to 1939 a far greater vintage than the period which led up to them.

Consider the Hispano-Suiza, which had developed from the promising old King Alfonso banger into that lovely thing as shining and as shapely as a sword.

Every proportion, from every angle, was absolutely right. Its radiator was knife-edged from the front and inches broad from the side, and the lines flowed from it like music from the conductor's baton. It travelled with an air. Commissionaires hurried, cap in hand, to open doors when it stopped.

The Isotta Fraschini ran it a close Italian second. A brilliant motorcar, with an added touch of massiveness and exhaust noise.

The Chapron Delages were already abroad in the land. There is no question that these were, from the point of appearance, the loveliest motor cars ever made, except for the one with the Figoni body which I myself subsequently possessed. But more of that anon. I remember the advertisements in the French newspapers. '*Silencieuse elle passe. C'est une Delage!*' And that most extraordinary one of all time, 'Regard the balance of masses.'

They were, indeed, sculptural. Imagine the makers of the average modern car taking a whole page in a newspaper to regard the balance of masses. But the other day I read an article in Lord Montagu of Beaulieu's magazine, *Veteran and Vintage*. The writer was enthusiastic about the old four-cylinder Delages, and dismissed the straight-eight as unworthy of comment. This is sheer obscurantism. As well wax enthusiastic about a leggy flapper of the twenties and dismiss Marlene Dietrich.

Which leads me to the German cars. There was a magnificent-looking machine called the Horch, which I fancy was the ancestor of the N.S.U. five-ring brigade. Whether it was any good or not I have no idea, because, naturally, like every other German car, it was completely eclipsed by the Mercedes.

By 1938 when Hitler and Goering were being driven

about in them, the Mercedes had evolved from a
black, knife-edged monstrosity running on alcohol in
the streets of Berlin, with that frightful tin hood-cover,
into a car fit for a dictator.

It is curious that in those nine years of the greater
vintage, the designers of every nation fully understood
that, for the lithe look, and the powerful look, or the
impressive look, or indeed any look worth looking at, a
car *has* to sit down behind its front, so to speak, just
as a ship must stream away from behind its prow.

The Mercedes boys knew this, but they added a
note of arrogance with the vast bonnet, the colossal
lamps, and the searchlights on either side of the
windscreen and, most of all, those flexible exhaust
pipes. They made the perfect setting for a rapt lunatic
to stand up with his arm at the Nazi salute. The
Mercedes was always well made. Second to the best, I
would say. But the most sensational phenomenon from
this factory was their SK Two Twenty.

My friend Conor Carrigan, whom you met briefly
at St-Jean-de-Luz, bought one of these monsters. It
was painted pure white. The Mercedes is the only
car which can wear pure white, though a great many
of those young men who push their Cortinas along in
shirt-sleeves would disagree with me.

This machine flaunted three gargantuan three-inch
flexible copper exhaust pipes emerging from either side
of the bonnet and disappearing somewhere underneath, and it had a supercharger which came in when
the right foot was in approximately the 'kick-down'
position of the modern automatic gear-box.

I drove it down the Portsmouth Road, and it was the
experience of a lifetime. With its high gearing and its
perfect smoothness it was surprisingly gentle without
the supercharger. But somewhere on the gentle slope

from Cobham by the old Brooklands turning down to Wisley, where we had been wuffling along at almost sixty, Conor said, 'Push it along, mate.' So I put my foot right down.

It was cataclysmic. The supercharger made a noise which rose in the chromatic scale of an air-raid siren, and the car jumped as if released by a spring. The faster we stormed the higher rose that maniacal howl, until, a mile away, the entire traffic in both directions dived for the ditch and we went through them like Boadicea, with peels of lunatic laughter and a blast of exhaust echoing in our wake.

That was heady stuff. So, in their ways, were the Duesenberg and the Cord, both of which sported flexible exhaust pipes, but, being American, were as quiet as mice.

The Cord I never liked much. In the first place it had front-wheel drive, which must be wrong when you come to think of it. The drive must be where the weight-transference takes place. Accelerate at the back and brake at the front is the motto. Personally I thought it was ugly, after the manner of Swedish furniture. But the Duesenberg was a classic car. I saw some body designs for it when I was in America. The bonnet was continued back over the top of the steering wheel and the windscreen was inches in front of the driver's face. Nasty if you hit something, but they looked marvellous, with the beauty in motion of the old Pacific locomotive, which the conductor couldn't see over at all and had to drive by peering along the side.

The nearest English equivalent of that shape was the six-litre Bentley. As a Swiss bystander once exclaimed when he beheld the engine of my old Phantom Continental, '*Quel morceau de puissance!*' What a chunk

63

of power! But we mustn't get led astray. We can't allow this catalogue of the aristocracy, this Almanach de Gotha, to omit the Packard Twin-six, or the Cadillac Sixteen. And the English contribution to this parade of magnificent motor cars, apart from the six-litre, were the other Bentleys, the Rolls Phantoms I and II and II Continental, followed by the twelve-cylinder Phantom III, and W.O. Bentley's Lagonda Twelve.

There is absolutely no possible shadow of doubt that those nine years, before war once again overtook us, will take their place in history as the crowning period of the petrol-driven machine. Think of the coachbuilders. Thrupp and Maberly. Freestone and Webb. Park Ward. Barker. Mulliner. Mann Egerton. Rippon. Hooper. Kellner. Figoni. Farina. Saoutchic. Ghia.

So now we come to it. I bought a Delage.

But not before an illicit and temporary liaison with a Daimler Fifteen.

In 1933, Daimler's decided the time had come to abandon the sleeve-valve principle, and that if they wanted to compete with their rivals they had to go over to poppets. If you can't beat 'em, join 'em. So they broke out with the very pleasant little Fifteens, with the fluid flywheel, the Wilson gearbox, a small six-cylinder push-rod overhead-valve engine, and remarkably pretty bodies by Mulliner. This applied particularly to the coupé, which had the fashionable trunk at the back with a fifth wire wheel behind it.

Though it was many years now since I used to flash through Esher in my Weymann Amilcar, the body designers were at last coming to the conclusion that, since you no longer had to climb up into a car, it was clear that the running board had better go. Fortu-

64

nately they didn't think of going all out for the slab side which is with us today. At least they allowed a wing to mark the transition between a round wheel and the necessarily straight line of a car's underneath.

The non-running-board wing appeared in a number of shapes. There was the purely motorcycle type wing which was fixed to the front axle and went up and down with the wheel. If I remember, this was taken up by the front-drive Alvis, the Blue Train Rover and the M.G.s, together with a number of sporting types, like the Frazer Nash and the Aston Martin, all of which were nice to look at and fun to drive.

The other sort was the helmet wing, which had a ridge running along the top and following through, down to what I can only describe as the 'neck piece'. It really did look very much like a helmet, and at that very moment, all unbeknown to me, the craftsmen at Figoni's in Paris were craftily fashioning a couple to fit the Delage which subsequently became mine. And in another place, wherever it was that Messrs Freestone and Webb had their *ateliers*, British craftsmen were doing precisely the same thing for the Rolls-Royce which I acquired about twenty years later!

The Daimler's wings were a genteel compromise between the helmet and tradition. They simply flowed down and back to where the running board would have started, and then tucked themselves modestly underneath. The whole thing looked very much like a Napoleonic carriage, and I took it to a coachbuilder and got him to give it a 'coach-line' by painting the doors and the underside at the back in ivory white. The effect was most successful, with the black trunk, the black leathercloth roof, and the navy blue bonnet and wings.

It made me feel like a film star, but the car had some 65

faults, forgivable, perhaps, in the first of a new
generation. The Wilson gear-box and the fluid flywheel,
all of cast iron, were heavy, far too heavy for anything
less than 3,000 cc. The only way to get any acceleration from a standstill, across a busy traffic artery, for
instance, was to rev the engine up to its limit with the
clutch down, and then remove the foot from it altogether.

Another severe disadvantage was that the chassis
was hopelessly whippy. Any sort of hole in the road
would twist it like a corkscrew, so that the radiator
quivered, the bonnet rattled and groaned, the doors
creaked and occasionally opened wide, and passengers
would tend to ask if anything was the matter.

So, as I said before, I bought a Delage.

CHAPTER IV

The Delage

I WILL TRY my best not to be lyrical. The body was by Figoni, who observed the same general proportions as Chapron, but added something which I can really only describe as solidity. The later Chapron bodies on the later Delages showed more than a trace of feminine tartiness. That, I suppose, was decadence. This one represented the golden age; it was made in 1929.

I will do my best to describe it without becoming bizarre. Seen from the front the radiator was chest-high, flanked in the French, high-bosomed Empire style by two enormous Grebel headlights, and all

67

three—the radiator and the phares—were protected by wire mesh with a neat chromed frame. The windscreen was quite remarkably narrow. It cannot have been more than a foot high, and it had the good manners to follow exactly the line of the top of the radiator and bonnet without rounding any corners. The wings were of very deep section and you could guess that they were helmet-shaped. One thing there was no need to start guessing about was the really vast Grebel spotlight staring at you by the driver's window. It was all of eighteen inches in diameter, on a swivel. As for the balance of masses, the front view was, broadly speaking, square, but the lower mass —radiator, bumper, tyres, in other words everything below the waistline—was five times everything above it.

The effect was dynamic, but the lines were so fine and so beautifully balanced that, in spite of its size, the impression was of an almost airy grace, and it was a great joy to the owner to hear the respectful chorus of 'Ah!' from the people who saw him coming. There was a Member of Parliament, I remember, coming out of St Stephen's, who took off his hat and stood cradling it to his breast like an American President saluting the flag.

Now come round with me to the side. There are certain proportions here that must be observed in my opinion, if one is setting out to design a beautiful car. The line of the radiator is set just slightly back of the front axle. This gives an air of lightness entirely at variance with the modern crudity of building in about three feet of frontal overhang. The windscreen rises, absolutely vertically, at a point precisely half way between the axles. The rear of the hood—it is a single-window drophead—is again defiantly vertical and

68

drops precisely to the centre of the rear wheel. The
top of the hood slopes gently upwards for two-thirds
of its length, and then slopes more rapidly downwards
to windscreen height again, or possibly slightly less,
and the falling line is accentuated by the tumble of the
chromed hood-irons. The wings are, indeed, helmet.
They follow exactly the circularity of the wheel and
at the correct artistic moment sweep backwards in the
general direction of the horizontal. The rear wings
are interchangeable, the relationship between the
superstructure and the body is about one to four and
a half; and as the whole conception, with a cavernous
boot plus the two spare wheels tucked on at the back,
approaches twenty-seven feet, the long low lines are
eye-catching beyond the power of words.

All the same I must say a few words about the
waistline, because it was this, to my mind, which set the
Figoni even above the Chapron. You really need to
crawl along an iron girder or something and look
downwards to understand the full artistry. If you can
manage this, you'll notice how the waistline begins
at the shoulder of the radiator, and widens in a perfectly straight line to meet the width of the windscreen,
which is already nearly the full width of the car. But
not quite. And now, my masters, still following exactly
the same line, the widening carries on. The backs of
the doors are wider than the fronts. The line of the
hood is wider than the windscreen.

Whereas the front wings have quite a massive
valance, the body is already over half the rear wings.
And—this is the touch of genius—the widening carries
straight on over the length of the boot for three feet or
so, which by now is the full width of the car. From
above the bodywork is perfectly dart-shaped. The
Chapron body didn't do this. It flattened at the doors

and narrowed at the boot, and though it was enormously elegant, and both he and Figoni had that
wonderful tumble-away at the back, I still think that
both of them were a heck of a lot better than the
spavined, or coke-bottle, tinware which the masses
drive in their shirtsleeves today.

That formidable length of bonnet wasn't all bonnet.
A quarter of it was scuttle, to bring that narrow
windscreen closer to the eye. And that reminds me.
This car had the cleverest windscreen wiper I ever met.
I cannot think why they don't make them today. Instead of whipping back and forth in an irritating arc,
this one approached vertically from the right and,
travelling upright, arrived at the centre of the screen,
and then wiped back again. There was another blade
which lived in the middle and wiped the passenger's
side. The really brilliant thing was that in bad conditions such as snow, you twiddled a knob, and *both*
blades travelled back and forth in front of the driver.

Its only disadvantage was that it worked through the
inlet pipe. So did the brakes. The wiper didn't matter
so much, since there was so much throwaway power in
the engine that the right foot could always find enough
juice to work the wiper. The brakes were another
matter. They were Clayton-Dewandre vacuum servo.
Our house at Peaslake, in which I still live, is served
by an extremely steep driveway with a right-angle
turn at the bottom. It was the easiest thing in the world
to start a cold engine, coast down the hill, allow the
engine to die, and find you were entirely without
brakes of any kind at the bottom. The only thing to do
was to slam in bottom gear, pull out the choke, yank on
the handbrake and offer up a silent prayer.

When that straight-eight engine was puffing away
it was the nicest engine I've ever sat behind, except the

V-8 I'm driving now. It's true that you need a straight six for perfect balance—always something moving up for something coming down—but for overlapping power impulses the eight cylinders deliver a steady stream right down to the lowest revolutions. This all makes for effortlessness. The Delage Eight was not particularly fast by modern standards (a top speed of about 87 mph), but its torque was fantastic.

Those were the days of Adolf Hitler, and as my father was anxious to catch sight of him and even, perhaps, gain an interview, I offered to drive him to Munich.

I took the opportunity to get my garage lengthened by six or seven feet while we were away, and once again we were hoisted aboard at Newhaven. The road to Germany took us through the old battlefields from where my father sent his dispatches in the First World War. We slid among miles and miles and miles of graves. I remember slipping along at a pleasant 65 mph when we spotted a rather ugly red monument. We stopped and walked over to see what it was. It simply said, in French, of course:

VERDUN

TO

THE

400,000 DEAD

Just one battle, and the dead of just one side.

So we sidled into Munich and parked the Delage outside a most elegant hotel with an unpronounceable name, the Vierjahreszeiten, which means 'The Four Seasons'. There was an extremely pretty girl there who clapped her hands together when she saw the Delage standing in the sunshine beneath a tree, with its very pale, very stippled grey metallic paint and its thin scarlet line, and cried '*Ah! Das ist ein farht wagen!*' 71

It was difficult not to call it the fart wagon after that. I always wonder what happened to that girl. I expect we killed her with the R.A.F.

We ate some tea with a lot of éclairs, and strolled out to look around. There was a longish, straightish street, with tramlines down the middle and trees along the side, and the good people of Munich seemed to have gathered on either hand as if they were expecting something to happen.

Presently an immense white Mercedes, of the dictatorial sort, bore slowly into view, with a great big man in a pure white uniform standing up in the back doing the Nazi salute.

'My God,' said my father, 'it's old Goering!'

A forest of arms went up as the car drove the last few yards and drew in to park immediately behind the Delage. At once the Mercedes was besieged, mostly by young women with flaxen hair and peasant blouses, and Goering continued to stand but bent down to them affably and spent the next half-hour signing autographs.

Goering had a rather more specialist taste in young women. There was a restaurant and nightclub attached to the Vierjahreszeiten called the Walterspiel, and my bedroom window was immediately on top of the canopied entrance to this place. The Delage was just to one side where I could keep an eye on it.

There were lovely warm summer evenings, and every night at about ten o'clock the white Mercedes would arrive and park just behind, with old Goering sitting among an absolute flowerbed of young females in evening dress, who squealed and tootled with laughter when the Reichsmarshal pinched their bottoms as they went through the door.

72 We never saw Hitler. At least I never did, because I

had promised to meet my wife in Paris after four or five days. My father decided to stay on, still hoping for an interview which would give him some inkling into Nazi intentions. So I pointed my beautiful car towards the West; and the very day I did so, my father went into the lounge at teatime, and there were Hitler, Goebbels, Himmler and Goering, all guzzling éclairs like men in a hurry.

I've told this story before in another book, but it bears repeating.

The thought came to my father that if only he had a revolver he could eliminate the entire bunch and do the world a bit of good.

While he was thinking this an American woman came back in through the swing doors and raised a raucous voice. Something about postal cards.

'Well, where *are* my postal cards? Did I or did I not buy a pack of postal cards right at this counter a quarter-hour ago? That's right. Well I'm telling you, I'm not quitting this place until somebody finds my postal cards!' And so on.

The waiters and the reception clerk and a sort of Junior Manager were very polite. They started moving cushions, and putting their hands down at the backs of chairs. It was at this point that a waiter with a white jacket and scarlet epaulettes came up with something which he held up in distaste, like a wet fish. It was a loaded revolver.

Ah well. Paris. And there was my wife waiting for me at the Napoleon. And there was Rex Harrison having his lighter filled with scented petrol at the bar. And there was that marvellous challenge, the passage of the Place de la Concorde, which, if you don't know what you are doing, can whiten the hair in a single minute, but if you do know what you are doing, is like 73

fencing, or like darning, or like a fugue by Bach. All
you have to do is let everybody who is coming from
the right whip through in front, and pay not the slightest attention to anybody on the left, even if he is
bearing down on you at 40 mph.

This is known as *la règle du droit*, the rule of the right,
and it's extremely difficult for an Englishman, born
and bred in the tradition that side roads are sub-
servient to main roads, not to forget. We motored
across France to the Cap d'Antibes in one go—the
Delage was marvellous at a steady 65—and turned into
the broad Avenue du Cap. There, across the end, was
the white hotel. Journey's end. With some exuberance
I trod on the accelerator. And at precisely that moment
a beastly small Fiat emerged from some crack in the
hedge at full tilt and careered straight across our bows,
which it was perfectly entitled to do. We went slap
into it. Wham!

There was a pregnant moment of indecision, then,
very slowly as it seemed, all four wheels tilted to
assume the horizontal, the Fiat lowered itself gently to
the ground, and out climbed seven or eight nuns, all
with fishing rods.

Mlle Paul, the receptionist, rushed out at the sound,
followed by the owner, M. Sellars, and a roadside
haggle arose in frantic French as to the amount of
damages I should have to pay. Nobody seemed to
want to embroil me in this, so I reversed the Delage
out of the Fiat, made a half circle round it, and drove
into the courtyard of the hotel.

The front of the Delage was absolutely unmarked.
The bill for the Fiat was F400. M. Sellars must have
been a clever man. Those holy nuns must have been
absolute saints. In those days bumpers were made for
bumps.

74

I kept that car for five whole years, the longest love affair I ever had, save one. On the way home we did what I used to consider that very caddish thing in the days of the Austin Swallow. We decided to beat the Blue Train.

There was absolutely nothing in it. We set forth at about ten—I hate early starts—crossed the Alps by the *Route Napoleon* with, far down below, another Delage creeping round the hairpin bends, lunched in Grenoble, dined in Orléans, and arrived in Dieppe at 1.30 in the morning with cracking headaches, but triumphant.

It was the war which separated us. Almost the last I remember of the Delage was driving my father to watch Mr Chamberlain come back from his visit to Hitler. The whole scene remains photo-clear in my head. We knew he was coming, and which way. One or two cars had already pulled up at the side of the road, waiting. The Delage joined them, with the hood down so that we could stand up and see. As the minutes ticked by other cars pulled up, and people arrived on foot. In half an hour there was quite a sizeable crowd, and the police had difficulty in keeping the road open.

Then there was a noise of horns down the road. People were happily beeping. Almost as one man the crowd surged into the road, and there was Mr Chamberlain, birdlike, in the back of an open landaulette. He had to stop. There was a roar of cheering and everybody pushed the horn-button. The Delage had three horns with a button for each, on which I could play simple tunes. I played like mad *Three Blind Mice*, and Mr Chamberlain stood up and began saying something. Nobody could hear a word he said but he waved a piece of paper, and after some minutes of this

75

the police managed to break a way for him, and he
drove off to that standing ovation in the House of
Commons.

A year later the war still hadn't quite come, though
it was obviously very close. We were in Cambridge,
staying with my in-laws. We felt that if there was to be
bombing we ought to return to base. So we piled the
luggage into that shapely boot and drove slowly back
to Surrey.

That was the last journey I made in her. There was
going to be a war, to which I might have to go. In any
case there was going to be petrol rationing. So I sold
her in exchange for a Sunbeam Talbot Ten coupé.

CHAPTER V

To
America

THE TALBOT TEN was a very dainty little car, with
rather a dainty motion. After the Delage the steering
seemed incredibly light, and one drove with one finger
each side of one of the spokes of the wheel. The engine
was remarkably smooth and quiet and eager, and it
would skip along at 55 mph for as long as one wanted.

I didn't keep it very long because we were now at
war and there was the problem of the refugee children.
My parents had a largish house and were obviously
about to have six or seven thrust upon them. Our house
was not so large, and the plan was that if my parents
moved across into it, we could make out a reasonable 77

case that the house was full. My mother offered her house for a convent of nuns who were anxious to escape from Streatham. This worked very well for a time but we now had far too many cars.

My mother was driving about in a clumsy great thing called an Austin Big Twelve. My wife had a rather nice little Austin Seven I had given her, with a foldaway roof. And I had the Sunbeam Talbot. So my mother and I agreed that we would put in both the Sunbeam Talbot and the Big Austin Twelve in exchange for a Sunbeam Talbot Two Litre which we could both use. The Two Litre lasted precisely two days.

It was bitter winter weather and I drove both my wife and my mother up to London through a blinding snowstorm. It was silly of us, really, to set forth like this but we were younger in those days, and we arrived.

When the time came to go home, the sky was black with snow, and when we left the London streets, which the traffic kept reasonably clear, we found the Kingston By-pass under about four inches.

Everybody travelled with the greatest possible care at about 20 mph leaving as long a distance as possible between the vehicles. When we got to the place where the road crosses the railway bridge we were all moving in a perfectly sensible convoy. Our car was the third in this little procession.

Then, for some unaccountable reason, the front car stopped. Dead. The second car went into the back of it. I realized that I wasn't going to be able to stop either, but I managed to skitter to a standstill by turning left on to the grass verge. Then a lady in a fur coat got out of the first car. To this day I cannot imagine why. Seconds later, while I was still wondering, I received a colossal thump from behind, and we were carried irresistibly forward. We bowled over the lady in the fur coat whose husband, fortunately, turned out to be a doctor, and there was then a chain reaction of fifteen or twenty cars behind, bumping into each other, the last one of which slithered dramatically sideways and ended up with its two front wheels over the edge of the railway bridge.

It was quite obvious that no one was going to sort that one out in the foreseeable future, so, after a general conference, we all made our way in a body to some railway station and after a bit of telephoning for taxis, went home by train.

The next morning I went off in the Austin Seven, with its handle tinkling musically, to the disaster area. Cars were still all over the place as if they had been strewn out of a pepperpot. The poor old Talbot, or perhaps I should say the poor young Talbot in its rather pleasant shade of pale green, was well and truly riven at the back. I won't say it was a write-off but it was quite obvious that a great many things had been bent, including the chassis. My feeling is that if a car has had that sort of thing done to it and it is going to be driven again, someone else had better do the driving. So having got into the Sunbeam Talbot habit of mind (rather like the period of the Renault) we part exchanged it for a three-litre Talbot sports saloon.

I liked that car. Though old enough not to have had the word Sunbeam tacked on to the word Talbot, it had the same attractive Sunbeam Talbot lines with a nice falling roof, elegant wings and a most attractive back view, with the spare wheel cover half recessed into the boot lid. It was painted black and it gleamed, and when I took it to America it caused an absolute sensation.

This was after about one year of war. I had been

out to France as a War Correspondent and had various adventures which you must read about in another book.

At the end of that year some horrible things had happened. The British Expeditionary Force had been totally defeated and had straggled out of Dunkirk. My mother had died with awful suddenness. France was in ruins. The Battle of Britain was going full blast. I had an inner conviction that somebody had better go and get help.

So I cooked up a little scheme with the Director General of the Ministry of Information that I should cross the Atlantic and try and get the Americans to enter the war.

I had roots in America, since two of my uncles, one an author and the other a dramatist, were living over there and had become American citizens. This meant that I could take my wife and my two children, knowing there would always be somewhere for them to live. But already the dead hand of the Treasury was making it impossible to get money out of the country and the only thing to do was to take with us everything we had. And that included the Talbot.

We went across in one of those deplorable convoys. I have no idea who dreamed this enormity up but there we were, forty-six ships in tight formation travelling at the speed of the slowest, which happened to be at exactly six knots. Of course we made a sitting target since the German U-boat of the period could comfortably exceed that speed underwater.

Nothing happened for about five days, and then to my horror we met a convoy coming in the reverse direction with destroyers ahead and aeroplanes in the sky above, and for half an hour or so there were no less than ninety-six ships in an area covering the marine equivalent, whatever that may be, of about four acres.

That night it happened.

There was a dullish thud, rather like the noise one makes running into a submerged tree trunk in a punt. Then another. And another. Ships were going down all around us. It was the most fantastic thing I ever saw. God knows what happened to all the people because the convoy didn't stop. It plunged ahead at six knots in a mindless sort of way like a herd of wounded animals who keep running.

Well, we got through. It was the other chaps who died. After sixteen days we made it and tied up at a pier in New York City. And there was the Talbot looking rather distressed, with two flat tyres and an empty battery, standing on American soil.

It was evident that we couldn't leave in her as we had intended, so I put the family on a train to Boston, booked a room in a hotel for myself and arranged to have the car put in order. I also, of course, had to visit, rather formally, the headquarters of the British Information Services in the British building to one side of Radio City in the Rockefeller Plaza.

There was a very charming Etonian there with the right tie and good manners who put me on to what he called the 'Schools and Colleges Division'. This suited me fine because Massachusetts and its surrounding country is packed with schools and colleges. There is Harvard, there is Yale and there is the Massachusetts Institute of Technology, and there is Boston University and Milton Academy, and in fact an absolute host of places of learning.

So it came to pass that the very next day I collected the Talbot, now gleaming again, with two American tyres on its wheels and two American six-volt batteries under its bonnet.

To an Englishman accustomed to the battle to
escape from London the ease of escape from New York
seemed positively astonishing. All you have to do is to
go down any of the side streets which cross Fifth
Avenue in a westerly direction and carry on across all
the other Avenues until you come to the river. The
first thing I noticed in doing this was the very sensible
system of traffic lights, which have still not been copied
in London thirty years later. The drill, if you are
stopped at a light, is to wait for it to turn green and
then, if you proceed at about 30 mph, which is a very
reasonable speed, you will find that all the lights turn
green for you as you arrive. They are interconnected.
They are phased. The result is that you get a perfectly
clear run and in minutes are on the thing called the
Merritt Parkway.

This is a remarkable engineering achievement. It is
built out on struts over the water of the West River and
it is what the Americans call 'landscaped'. Trees have
been planted and lawns sloped down to it, and for this
purpose whole blocks of houses have been moved
back. There is one complete hospital which was moved
back twenty feet to allow for the lawns and trees in
front of it.

On the road itself all the traffic moves at precisely
the same lighthearted clip. Nobody passes anybody
else. There is no sense of competition whatever. You
don't come across the young man in the Ford Cortina.
All American cars have eight-cylinder engines of about
the same size. They all have the same acceleration and
the same potentialities for speed and the whole lot
proceed in solid formation.

The result of all this is that at the end of half an
hour, instead of finding oneself stationary on, say,
Putney Bridge, you have left New York a good twenty

miles behind and are storming along in the open
country.

I say 'storming' along. This is not strictly true. The Americans are not fast drivers and speed limits are very rigidly enforced. It seemed to me that we took pretty well everything at a steady 65 mph, but when there are no crossroads or holdups of any kind whatever the way in which the miles are eaten up is remarkable.

The Talbot was perfectly at home in this company. As I say, it created a sensation. People hung their heads out and peered and waved through their back windows. Quite a number of people lowered their glass and yelled over.

'Say, what kind of a car is that?'

'It's a Talbot.'

'Yeh? She certainly is good-looking.'

This was all very satisfactory. Boston, I think, is something like 300 miles from New York. Following the coastline of Connecticut through some of the most charming villages I had ever seen, with their white painted houses and their giant American elms and the Christopher Wren churches, I made it in about four and a half hours with absolutely no trouble at all.

Did I say 'absolutely no trouble at all'? Three days later the Talbot was limping like a cat on three feet. I took it to the neighbourhood garage which was full of cheerful souls in white coats with their christian names emblazoned in semicircles on the back. 'Bunny'. 'Tiny'. 'Spike'. They clustered round the Talbot.

'Old-timer, huh?'

Already the American car had lost its separate head-lamps and wore them embedded in the front wings. They opened the bonnet.

'Gee, take a look at the thickness of this metal! Like a truck!'

83

They diagnosed burnt exhaust valves.

I had brought a set of spare valves with me in case this sort of thing occurred. They whipped them in in no time at all.

'Gee tanks,' I said, already learning the American lingo.

'It's a pleasure,' said Bunny, and Tiny, and Spike.

Three weeks later, after some fast drives round Massachusetts to keep my speaking engagements, the same thing happened again.

Bunny shook his head and explained that American petrol was highly leaded and that old-fashioned metals didn't stand up to it. There was one Service Station in the town which sold unleaded petrol; he suggested that I took my custom there. I said I didn't think this was any good. It might save the thing happening a second time but it wouldn't make new valves grow where there were burnt valves before.

He had an idea that he might be able to grind down some Hudson valves to fit. Did I want him to try? It would take a day or two and he could lend me a Hudson to tide me over.

This sounded like a sensible scheme and I drove home in a fast, unsightly, eight-cylinders-in-line, side-valved, splash-lubricated bar parlour.

I must admit I was unpatriotically impressed. The steering of this gigantic beast was silken. Its engine, unchanged in design over twenty years, was as silent as a ghost. It was its suspension which really made me open my eyes.

The Talbot rather fancied itself in this respect. It had a large lever on the right of the dash, working on a sort of vertical quadrant by which you could alter the setting of the shock absorbers as you went along.

84 On the main road this worked well enough, because

you could accommodate to the number of passengers TO AMERICA in the car. But there was one place I remember, behind the waterworks in Taunton, where the road was rutted and potholed to such a disgraceful degree that the poor old Talbot shuddered and shook like the Austin Swallow. It never entered my head that any car in such conditions would not do the same. When I took the Hudson over it we travelled with absolutely no sensation of any sort whatsoever. I was so amazed that I went back and did it again. I was aware, this time, that the wheels were pattering and dancing about, but the body of the car seemed completely divorced from the wheels, and proceeded with absolutely no deviation from the horizontal.

Later, I discovered that all American motor cars had learned this trick. They called it 'the boulevard ride' and I have to confess that I don't know myself how it's done; nor, apparently, does any English manufacturer. It must have something to do with an enormously strong, unflexing chassis, a weight of approximately two tons, very soft springs and shock absorbers which somehow or other reduce their periodicity rate to something in the nature of three seconds. Three days later I got the Talbot back, and I never had another mite of trouble from the valves. I take my hat off to that old Hudson.

The Hudson wasn't an expensive car. On the contrary, it was the elder brother of the Essex, and that was in about the same class as the new Model A Ford. Yet its engine was used to power such fastidious motor cars as the Brough Superior and the Railton, just like the Chevrolet which finds itself at the heart of some extremely exotic motoring today.

Well, the Japanese did my job for me. I was on my way to give a lecture at a place called Pittsfield, with the 85 radio playing in the car. It was then I heard the news of Pearl Harbor. It wasn't very much use doing my tear-jerking stuff about the blitz in London, and little Bobby dead in his mother's arms as Mr Churchill arrived to give the V sign. So I turned straight round and went home. This was the point at which the question of money raised its ugly head. I had been allowed to bring a small amount of money with me. I had been doing the job free except for occasional expenses. Anyhow, the job was over. When the people allowed me to bring the car out, it was on condition that I brought it back again. I had to give a promise not to sell it in the United States, so that was out. I simply didn't have the fare for four people home and it didn't seem as if either of my uncles had either.

CHAPTER VI

An Englishman and his Buick in Hollywood

I HAD READ that Zoltan Korda, an old friend of mine, was in Hollywood. So I sent him a telegram.

'Stuck Massachusetts without a sausage. S.O.S.'

Zoli behaved like an absolute angel. He wired me the plane fare to Hollywood. When I arrived, wild-eyed and sleepless (in those days the journey took sixteen hours) he put me in a hotel, paid my bill once a week, got me a job as a scriptwriter in Twentieth Century Fox and said, 'Now you can pay me back.'

I did too. I had to earn something like $4,000, over and above our living expenses to get the family home, but the good Fox people poured money all over me. I   87

took a flat, sent for the family to come out by train,
and bought a Buick.

That Buick was a 1943 model, almost new, and it
had several features which had not yet appeared on the
other side of the Atlantic. In the first place it had
flipping blinkers instead of the blinking flippers we
were all accustomed to. These were very amusing to
operate as you raised a lever and a very nice little
chiming sound came from somewhere to remind you to
move it back. It also had lights on stalks and you
started the engine by turning the ignition on.

In that year, the Americans had developed the 'Pay
as you go' system to a point which it hasn't yet reached
in this country. There was no deposit to pay and the
monthly charge was quite preposterously low—$39.
Nobody asked any questions, nor did I have to give any
sort of bank guarantee or show that I was earning a
salary. I simply walked into the showroom and drove
out about ten minutes later. The fact is that anybody
buying a car under this arrangement was not really
buying a car at all. Americans don't run their cars for
more than a year or two, so at that rate of interest they
never actually possess the car. When they want something else, they simply turn up at the showroom,
choose the car they want, wait while a little arithmetic
is done to determine the difference in values between
the two cars, and start paying $39 a month to cover
that. Contrary to English understanding, American
cars never wear out. They simply decline in value until
they become worth about $25. You can buy them out-
right for that. A great many American college boys do.
I would be prepared to bet my bottom dollar that
somewhere or other that Buick is still going strong in
some incredible place, like the University of Kala-
mazoo.

When it was secondhand for the first time it still carried its showroom gleam. It had a broad grill rather like the modern Daimler Dart, low down in the front. Its headlamps, of course, were recessed into the wings, and the fastback I bought was remarkably successful.

It had a broad sofa seat inside, quite capable of carrying four people abreast, and then far away at the back in the diminishing tail there was a single seat, which I never knew anyone to occupy.

That car had the most astonishing low-speed torque I have ever encountered. My friend Zoli Korda lived with his wife and their little son, David, and an English nurse at the top of a rocky promontory called Look-Out Mountain. This was a lovely place. It was 3,000 feet high. To get to it you had to put the Buick at a succession of short, sharp zigzags of about one in eight. The eight-cylinders-in-line Buick engine would creep up this lot at about 6 mph in top gear with never a protest or falter. The first time this happened I could hardly believe it. The gear-change was on the steering wheel (another new-fangled notion), and I had my hand all ready to shift it to second. Not a bit of it. The car proceeded with complete serenity, purring like a pussy. When I got to the top there were two 1943 Buick Eights standing at the door. The other was Zoli's and it was on his recommendation that I had got mine.

That place is one of the nicest places I know. It was slightly spoilt by the presence of a broken lamppost, which Zoli assured me used to get its bulb shot out weekly so that lovers could pursue their devotions in the dark. There was also a Chinese woman who used to ride around on a scooter showing her stomach. I have never been a great admirer of the naked navel, and

I found this Asian example most distasteful. But those
were details. The view was staggering. At the back of
the house, towards the East, arid and somehow
reptilian and yet magnificent, peaks reached all the
way to the Arizona desert. From the front of the
house where the lamppost was, one looked down on
the whole mighty city of Los Angeles. Nobody will
believe me when I tell them this, but at night that view
is the most beautiful thing in the world. On the right is
the Pacific Ocean, with the red light of the setting sun
still faintly visible through the mist. There is always a
Pacific mist. Immediately down below is a fantastic
pattern of lights, moving lights, coloured lights,
stretching as far as the eye can see. Ridiculously
enough, it's the traffic. Swarms of cars all moving along
the throughways, the freeways, and every other sort of
way, crisscrossing, interlocking, swirling round clover-
leaf junctions. And all over the city there were traffic
lights changing colour from red to green to amber. You
never saw anything like it.

Zoli was awfully kind to me and so was his wife,
Joan, who used to be Joan Gardner. They had me up
to dinner several times a week when work was over,
and the Buick would climb up and down as if it had
got to know the way like a mule on a mule track. Then
the family arrived.

We took a flat on Wilshire Boulevard in the Los
Angeles suburb of Westwood. It was rather a poshish
flat as flats go, but we chose it because it was run by an
English woman. In the flat underneath was Johnny
Weismuller who played the part of Tarzan. In the
ground-floor flat underneath that Greta Garbo must
have known somebody, because she would come every
Thursday morning at about eleven o'clock, striding up
the path between the palm trees, in a long, ankle-length

dress and a floppy felt hat, looking very serious indeed.

One night I parked the Buick outside and went upstairs to kiss the children goodnight.

There was a sort of well in the middle of the building, to give light and air, and from across this well there was coming one hell of a noise from the flat opposite.

In that climate all the windows are always open and we could hear the nagging voice of a woman raging uncontrollably. 'Nag nag nag.' 'Wah wah wah.'

I'm afraid the children and I hung out of the windows listening. From time to time a man's voice would attempt to interrupt.

'Oh shut up! Shut up for Pete's sake, will ya?'

'Nag nag nag.' 'Wah wah wah.'

'If you don't stop that God-awful racket,' the man said, 'I'll stop it for you. I'm giving you fair warning.'

The woman's voice rose to a scream.

'O.K.,' said the man, 'take that!'

There was sudden disconcerting silence. We looked at each other. From some other flat a radio was playing 'Deep Purple'. But from the flat opposite not a single sound.

Somebody must have telephoned. In minutes the air was rent with the howling and screaming of the Police Pontiacs. It was the Homicide Squad. Minutes later a white Cadillac ambulance arrived screaming with its siren at full blast. Two people were taken away, one vertical, the other horizontal.

Next morning, a little shaken by the eruption of this violence, I went down after breakfast and got into the Buick to drive the few yards to the Fox Studio. In Hollywood you have to drive, you know. If you go for a walk they pick you up for vagrancy. I had hardly gone more than thirty or forty yards and was passing under the arch of one of the throughways when, with a noise like cannon fire, all four tyres exploded one after the other, Bang! Bang! Bang! Bang!

I crawled out and viewed the remains with dismay. The tyres were not only all punctured but they were all worn right through to the canvas. When I acquired the car all four had been virtually new.

Fortunately there was a garage just on the other side of the bridge, so I rolled towards it on the rims.

A man came towards me, grinning.

'It's the most fantastic thing,' I said. 'All four of my tyres exploded at once.'

He grinned more widely.

'Yeah. I heard it.'

'My tyres were practically new.'

'Could be. But those aren't your tyres.'

'Not my—?'

'Where do you park the car?'

'Just over there, in the forecourt.'

'All night?'

The idea dawned on me.

'Well I'm damned!'

'You said it, brother.'

'Do you mean to tell me that while I slept, some little man came along, jacked up each wheel in turn, took off the tyre, put on his own tyre, and then changed all my tyres onto his own rims? It would have taken him about four hours.'

'Oh no. Mostly they take the wheels too.'

'Well, for crying out loud!'

'That's right.'

'Well, can you put four new tyres on for me?'

'Brother, don't you read the papers? There's a war on.'

92   'Damn it, I know that.'

'There isn't a single new tyre to be had in the whole of Los Angeles. All taken by the military. All gone to help the war effort.'

'Well, what do I do?'

'The only thing I can think of is join the army.'

'Dash it all, this is America. There must be a black market somewhere.'

'Slip me fifty and I'll give you an address.'

I slipped him fifty.

He brought a piece of paper with oily fingermarks all over it, licked a stub of pencil and, leaning on the bonnet, wrote out an address. It was somewhere in downtown Los Angeles, near all the strip joints.

'Thanks,' I said. 'How do I get there without tyres?'

'Give me a couple of hours,' he said, 'and I'll fix these for you.'

So I had to walk on my own two feet to Twentieth Century Fox. Nobody picked me up for vagrancy. The cop at the gate looked a bit startled and made me show him some sort of card I carried before he would let me in.

'Somebody pinched my tyres,' I told him.

'Isn't that just too bad.'

I explained the situation to my secretary, who was an English girl called Muriel, and after the wonderfully good lunch supplied in the Fox Commissary, I walked back to the garage.

There stood the Buick proudly raised on all four wheels.

'Oh good!' I said. 'Do you think they'll stand up?'

'For about twenty miles, I reckon, if you keep the speed down. I've had to do quite a bit. I've vulcanized all the tubes and put in plenty of newspaper. It's the *Los Angeles Times*,' he added. 'Should be all right.'

I thanked him and slip-slapped off to downtown

Los Angeles. It's a sleezy place, and, if the streets
weren't about ten times as wide, it might have been
Soho itself. In its centre stands the Biltmore Hotel, of
once-fashionable antiquity.

I asked the chap at the door if he knew where the
place was.

He said, 'Yes, sir! Right around there.'

And so it was.

I walked in, bold as brass, and said, 'I've been
looking for four new tyres for a Buick Eight. I've been
given to understand you know where I could get
them.'

He looked at me very sharply indeed, but I think his
suspicions were allayed by the fact of my obvious
Englishness. Clearly I wasn't a cop, and it was improbable that I was a member of the F.B.I.

'Cost you plenty,' he said.

'How much?'

He wouldn't even mention the sum but drew the
figures in the air with his finger. It was about four
times the normal price.

Well I had to have four tyres. I asked him if he
would take a cheque.

'No, sir! Cash. What's your bank?'

'The Farmers,' I told him.

'Funny name for a bank.'

I could see a branch opposite from where we stood.
I walked across the street and came back with $160.

The man took them quietly and put them in his hip
pocket.

'Now be very careful and listen to me,' he said. 'I
want you to drive the car along Sunset Boulevard till
you come to the Wig Wag. Know the Wig Wag?'

I knew the Wig Wag very well. For some strange
reason known only to the Founding Fathers, Sunset

Boulevard and Wilshire Boulevard run parallel all the
way from central Los Angeles to the Wig Wag, where
they cross, only to run parallel once again to the coast
at Santa Monica. The crossing used to be bad enough
—I expect there's a bridge over it now—but the
situation was complicated by a train which would
occasionally add to the general confusion by arriving
with a large blast on its hooter and menacing clangs of
its bell. The appalling danger of this was signalled by a
strange contraption made of wood in the shape of a
clock's pendulum. This had a skull and crossbones
painted on the round bit at the bottom and, not to put
too fine a point upon it, it wagged.

'Fine,' the man said. 'Follow Sunset for half a mile
and you'll find a road forking to the right. In the
centre of the fork is a service station. Drive into the
Wash, and say you want the car simonized.'

So off I went, hoping and praying that thc tyres
would hold, and that I wouldn't have to buy four new
wheels on the black market as well. I found the
garage all right. It's very easy in American cities to
find one's way because the streets are all so parallel.
I drove on to the Wash, which, as you might imagine,
was a concrete place with a drain in the centre, and
sat quietly in the car waiting.

After some time a white coated attendant appeared.

'Yes?' he asked.

'I want the car simonized, please.'

He looked at the tyres.

'You can say that again, mister! Can you give me an
hour and a half?'

'I suppose so.'

'There's a drugstore just up the road. Get yourself
something to eat and come back at four o'clock.
Right?'

95

I didn't really want anything to eat, but I walked along in the pleasant sunshine and ordered a pot of tea. This rather shook them. The Americans on the whole don't drink tea, and when they do they put a tea bag into tepid water, serve it in a glass with two straws, and wonder what on earth the English see in it.

One and a half hours later I turned up again, and there was the Buick looking absolutely magnificent. It had been simonized. It shone with a transparent lustre. It was like looking into the depths of the sea off the coast of Bermuda. More important still, it had four perfectly brand-new tyres, and on each, in large raised letters painted white, were the words 'U.S. Army Only'.

'I done a good job, mister.'

'You certainly have. But couldn't you have put them the other way round with the lettering on the inside?'

He smiled faintly. I think he was an Irishman.

'You're in the Service now.'

He was absolutely right, of course. Nobody was going to steal those tyres.

I kept the Buick about a month longer before the Talbot turned up. I discovered an extraordinarily good system whereby young undergraduates who wanted to travel from New York to California would drive someone else's car, with no payment on either side. I never met the lad in question, but somebody drove it flat out for 3,000 miles, left it in front of our door, and crept away without making himself known. When I came out next morning to go to work, it was just standing there. My wife wasn't keen on driving the Buick. She said it was too big. So one of my jobs was to sneak away from the studios rather early—they

didn't mind a bit, so long as one turned in a reasonable

job in a reasonable time—and pick up my children from their two schools. My little girl, who must have been about four, went to a species of infant academy. Her name was Frances. Of course they called her Fraances. She was said to be studying 'Administrative Buildings'. In some ways the Americans are extraordinary people. In order to make myself understood I had to call her Fraances too. I went to fetch her one day, but couldn't see her anywhere so I asked an obvious mistress if she had seen Fraances.

'She's right over there,' said the mistress, 'doing creative work in the sandpit.'

I used to plonk her beside me in the car, and then both of us would go off to a gigantic establishment called the Ralph Waldo Emerson Junior High.

At about 4.30 a stream of the most repellent people would emerge, hairy Mexicans, dark-skinned Aztecs, scruffy characters in jeans and T-shirts, Chinamen, lots of Chinamen; in the middle of this outpour, my son Martin would suddenly appear with his hair carefully brushed, wearing a neat flannel suit with Harrods written all over it. I felt very sorry for him, but as a matter of fact he enjoyed it. One of the girls in his class had been divorced, which would have been considered unusual in an English school. One afternoon Martin told me, going home in the Buick, that a boy had knocked on the door, come into the classroom and said, 'Please, sir, may I get a cup of water?'

The master nodded.

Perhaps I should tell you that in every American classroom an enormous demijohn, or vat, of water stands in one corner, with a stack of disposable plastic cups underneath.

The boy went solemnly across, filled a cup rather full, and carried it delicately to the door.

97

Ten minutes later he was back.

'Please, sir, can I get a cup of water?'

The master was slightly more surprised this time, but again he nodded curtly, and once again the boy filled a cup to the brim and carried it, slowly and carefully, to the door.

Ten minutes later he was back for the third time.

'Please, sir, can I get a cup of water?'

'For the love of Pete!' exclaimed the master. 'What is all this? Don't you have any water of your own? And anyway what do you want with so much water?'

'Please, sir,' the boy said pathetically, 'the gym's on fire.'

Martin told me the whole class, together with the master, exploded into roars of hilarious laughter. I don't know—perhaps it was only appearances that were against them.

And then, as I told you, the Talbot arrived.

I took the Buick to the shop I'd bought it from and explained that my own car had put in an appearance and said I was terribly sorry but I wanted to stop buying the Buick.

The chap was argumentative. He relied on the desire of every right-minded American to change his car about once every year. How else could they cover the depreciation? Finally, he retired to a small office, where no doubt he consulted his pals. Finally he came out again all sleek and smiling and asked if I was prepared to pay an extra $39 to cover this item.

I didn't actually embrace him, but I thought, and still think, that to be able to hire a perfectly good eight-cylinder Buick for $39 a month was one of the brightest aspects of American civilization.

The old Talbot was looking a bit tatty after its 3000-mile drive, no doubt at 70 and 80 mph, through the

continent of America. Largely to see what would
happen, I took it along to my friend at the service
station just off Sunset Boulevard.

'I want a simonize, please,' I said.

He walked all round the car and then appeared
again at the window. He pushed up a white cap to
scratch his head.

'What's the matter with those, mister?'

'I want a simonize.'

'You want a simonize?'

'Yes, please.'

'Oh you want a *simonize!*'

'That's what I said. You did a beautiful job.'

I was sure he was an Irishman, when he grinned. He
had four very yellow teeth in the front of his mouth.

'O.K., mister! Three quarters of an hour this item.'

I made my way to the same drugstore. Seeing the
Hollywood movies in Hollywood, I had often watched
tough hombres push through the double doors and
say, 'Gimme a sarsaparilla'. Then the barman would
slide some evil-looking mixture fifteen feet along the
bar.

I said, 'Gimme a sarsaparilla, will ya,' in my best
Hollywood lingo.

There wasn't any sort of bar to slide anything along,
but a very pleasant young man, obviously a college
boy earning a bit in his spare time, leaned down
behind the counter, sloshed around a bit, said, 'One
sarsaparilla coming up', and slapped a glass with two
straws in front of me.

It was disgusting. It was jet black, flecked with
overtones of purple where the ice cream had touched
the glass. It tasted violently of liquorice and I trembled
to think what its aftereffects might be. Tough hombre
that I was, I got to the bottom of it, and then ordered

99

two cups of coffee to take away the taste. The smell remained. About three quarters of an hour later, to the dot, I showed up at the service station. There was my black beauty, resplendent once again. She looked as though she had just stepped two yards from Piccadilly.

The Talbot wouldn't go up Look-Out Mountain in top gear. It wanted second for the hairpins and third for the straights. But it looked elegant among the twenty-year-old Pontiacs and the Model A Fords owned by the undergraduates of U.C.L.A. (University of California Los Angeles).

As a matter of fact, there were quite a number of foreign cars in Hollywood. Pre-war open two-seater M.G.s were commonplace. One day I saw a beautiful Bentley with its hood half rolled up so that it looked like a *coupé de ville*. I had no idea who owned it. I only saw it once. There was also a stunning eight-cylinder Bugatti with an open body that flashed in and out of the traffic making a noise like 8000 mosquitoes. This kind of thing lent status.

It lent me status too, for a very short while. The cop at the gate of the Fox Studio, who had challenged me when I arrived on foot, saluted the Talbot smartly with a gleam in his eye. But I had finished the film and I had my $4,000 stashed away in the Farmers Bank. It was time to go.

The problem was, what to do with the Talbot. I must confess I didn't quite like the idea of crowding my wife and two small children into it and driving 3000 miles across the desert and all the rest of America, in high summer temperatures of around 90°. Rather rashly, I had given a promise to the man in London who allowed me to put it on the ship that I wouldn't sell the car in America.

100   Then someone told me there was a chap who

specialized in foreign cars, and liked to keep a show of them in the window, just for the look of it. When I arrived the Bugatti was standing in front. In the windows were a white S.S. 100 and an open four-and-a-half-litre Bentley, with the bonnet up so that you could see the engine shine.

I went in and was greeted by a Frenchman in a beret. I explained the situation. I told him I had to go back to England to finish the war, and would he aid the Allied effort by keeping it in his showroom until victory.

To my astonishment, he agreed instantly. He wanted to know what train I was catching.

I said I didn't know yet, but I rather thought of buying four tickets on *The Chief* in about three days' time.

'That's fine,' he said. 'Bring the Talbot here three quarters of an hour before the train goes and I'll drive you to the station in the Bugatti.'

'It's a deal,' I said. And we shook hands.

So I bought my tickets, said goodbye to the friends I had made, flashed through the traffic in the Bugatti, and, four months later, arrived in London. Not before I received a message from a friend of mine in Hollywood that the day after I had left, the chap who ran the foreign car showroom had decamped with the entire stock and crossed the border into Mexico. So I kept my promise, I didn't sell the car. I had it stolen.

CHAPTER VII

Meeting
Mr Paddon

THIS IS SUPPOSED to be a book about cars, so I won't dilate on the incredible transition from Californian sunshine to poor old battered, dirty, broken London, with its howling sirens, searchlights, barrage balloons, aeroplanes, anti-aircraft fire, and the hiss and thunder of the bombs.

This was really the lowest moment of the war. There was not the smallest sign of victory anywhere. There was nothing to eat. The women all walked about in bare legs, and there was no petrol.

My wife wanted to take the children to Cambridge where her parents lived. I couldn't do that except at   103 weekends, because I had a job in London. Since no-body could drive a car for more than a few miles a month because of the rationing, they were to be had at fantastically low prices. So I bought a car. It cost me £400. It was an absolutely brand-new 1939 Daimler Eighteen, a natural return to my old love, I suppose. Anyway it helped to cheer me up.

My goodness, those things had grown up since the days of my 1933 Fifteen. This model, I believe, was called, rather foolishly, 'The Ritz'. That was the standard steel saloon. This one had a distinctly agree-able four-door drophead body by Tickford. I think it was the only one made. It looked almost exactly like the dropheads Barkers had been building, except for the four doors. It was painted a nice metallic grey, just like my old Delage, with a thin red coach line and a tan top.

I heard word of a little place, somewhere in the Ladbroke Grove-Holland Park region, where there was a character who knew all about methanol. Methanol is pretty pure alcohol, without the water put in methylated spirit, and was used in the days when people still went motor racing, to mix with the petrol so that unutterably high compression ratios could be used. Unfortunately, being an alcohol, methanol didn't really mix with petrol. It was a question of shaking the bottle and keeping it shaken. That might be all right for a racing car doing 130 mph round a circuit, but for a staid Daimler on its way to Cambridge he didn't think it would work.

I told my character there must be some way of doing this. Otherwise why should I have been recom-mended to come to him?

The character looked left and right.

'Secret tank,' he said. 'Use fuel separately. Start
104 on petrol. Then switch over.'

So it was done. He welded up a great tank to hold
about twenty gallons which exactly fitted the inside of
the boot. Then he took a pipe to a tap, just underneath
the dashboard, which poured petrol one way and
methanol the other to the single carburettor.

Fortunately this was an S.U. I say, 'fortunately',
because methanol requires an immensely richer mixture, and the so-called choke on the S.U. carburettor is
not a choke at all, but alters the mixture by pushing
up a tapered needle into the air supply.

It worked absolutely perfectly! You switched over
to petrol, started the engine in the usual way with the
choke out, and when the engine was hot enough for the
choke to be pushed right home, then you switched
over to methanol and pulled it right out again. If you
were reasonably deft over this, the change was quite
imperceptible, and you proceeded merrily on your way,
without using any petrol at all.

I must explain that I had a job working for a newspaper in Gray's Inn Road, and this used to keep me
until dinner time on Saturday nights. That is, if I was
lucky. If I was not lucky and, say, Lord Montgomery
did something foolish, such as mounting a full-scale
invasion of Sicily, then one had to sit down and re-
write practically the whole paper, which would take
one until 1.30 in the morning. So it was always night
when the methanol took me to Cambridge to see my
family.

There was no trouble about parking, of course, in
those days. There were practically no cars to park. I
used to drive from the hotel, where I stayed during the
week, along empty streets to the big offices in Gray's
Inn Road, where I would simply leave the car in
front of the front door and enter in. At 7.30 or so,
when the first edition had gone to bed, I would drive

the Editor to the Ivy Restaurant, leave the car as usual
immediately in front of the door, and do my best to
escape the rigours of rationing.

If, during the meal, the Editor wasn't called suddenly to the telephone, we knew it was all right for me
to start the journey.

Except for buses and taxis and the odd car or two,
I would drive up through empty London, past Lords
to Hendon, heading for the Barnet By-pass. Once at
Apex Corner three American soldiers walked into the
beam of my headlamps, and jerked their thumbs in a
northerly direction. I pulled up.

'Hop in, fellas,' I said.

They hopped in.

'How far are you going?'

'Cambridge.'

'Say, isn't that swell. What kind of car is this?'

'It's a Daimler.'

'Come again?'

'A Daimler.'

'That's a new one on me. Ever heard of a Daimler,
Shorty?'

'Nope,' said Shorty. He was, of course, about six
foot five.

As we passed The Barn at Elstree, three more
American soldiers stepped into the lights.

'No more room, I'm afraid,' I said.

'Sure there's room! Hop in, fellas!'

So they hopped in, if you can call it hopping. It was
more of a slug-like motion. One of them sat on the lap
of the man beside me. That meant that four of them
had arranged themselves on the back seat. Don't ask
me how. All I know is that when one of them spoke I
could, literally, feel him breathing down my neck.

106 'Say, what kind of a car is this?'

Above: *1925
6-cylinder 40cv
Renault open tourer
with skiff body*
RENAULT

Left: *1925 6cv
Renault saloon*
RENAULT

Above left: *1926 14/40 Delage*
M.M.M.

Below left: *1927 14/40 Vauxhall saloon*
VAUXHALL

Above: *1927 4-cylinder 6cv Renault N.N. Torpedo de luxe*
RENAULT

Below: *1929 Mercedes–Benz drophead coupé*
D.T.C.L.

Inset: *1930 Cord L29*
M.M.M.

Left: *1930 6-cylinder 21 hp Renault coupé de ville*
RENAULT

Right: *Gertrude Lawrence in her La Salle V-8*
R.T.H.P.L.

Centre: *The Prince of Wales' visit to Reading University, 1926*
R.T.H.P.L.

Below: *Maurice Chevalier leaning over his radiator*
POPPERFOTO

Left: *1931 Delage D8*
M.M.M.

Below: *1931 Austin Seven Swallow*
B.M.C.

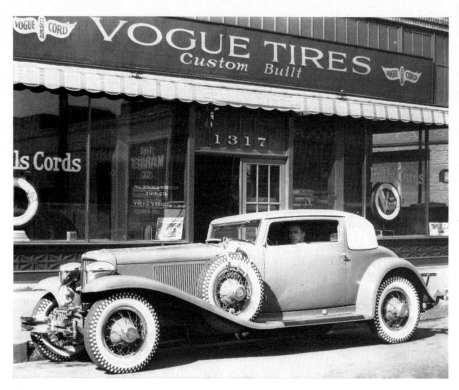

Above: *1931 Cord
L29 fixed head
coupé*
M.M.M.

Right: *1933 20–25
Rolls-Royce*
M.M.M.

'It's a Daimler.'

'Huh?'

'A Daimler. The internal combustion motor was invented by Herr Gottlieb Daimler.'

'Is that so?'

They went on discussing the car among themselves.

'What speed are we doing?'

'Sixty.'

'Sweet, isn't she! About the equivalent of a Lincoln, I reckon.'

'Not much pick-up, though.'

'What's the T for on that gear-shift?'

'Top,' I told them.

'You mean high?'

'That's right,' I said. 'We call it top.'

'Well, what do you know?'

These journeys began to conform to a pattern so that I cannot remember now t'other from which. One early morning, I know, I arrived in Cambridge with no less than seven American soldiers in the car. One day one of them pressed two half crowns into my sweaty palm. 'To help towards the gas,' as he explained.

They all came from a secret aerodrome just beyond Cambridge, which I was never allowed to see. They always trooped out of the car in the middle of Cambridge, saying that they had transportation. I believe it was one of the most extraordinary pieces of construction of the entire war. The whole place was phoney. The church slid away on rails. The houses collapsed like packs of cards. From underground hangars, great lifts appeared, bringing aeroplanes up to ground level.

The great thing about working for a Sunday newspaper is that you don't have to put in an appearance much before eleven o'clock on Wednesday mornings.

One morning I was bowling along at about 60 mph on that fast stretch which comes from Cambridge and turns into the Great North Road at Baldock. I had only two Americans from that secret place in the car. With extreme suddenness and without any premonitory wobble of any sort, the nearside rear wheel came off. Thank God it was a rear wheel. I jammed on the brakes as we came down on the rear drum. It must have taken the car something like 300 yards to stop, but the wheel bowled merrily ahead of us, still doing all of 60 mph. It leapt a shallow kerb, shot between two elderly ladies with parasols who were taking a little walk, flew over a low hedge and disappeared into a field of ripening corn.

While I was still blinking to get my senses back, the two American soldiers disappeared almost as rapidly as the wheel. I think they must have run. I didn't actually notice them go but when I turned to suggest that they might help me with the jack, they were not among those present. The two old ladies seemed hardly to have been aware of the event. They probably thought it was a dog or a cat or even, possibly, a pigeon or a bat scared by the crunching noise of the Daimler coming to a halt.

By the grace of God an A.A. man came up on his motor-bicycle, and he helped me trample down the farmer's field of corn before we could find the wheel and put it on again.

'How in the world did that happen, governor?'

I knew exactly how it had happened but I didn't tell him. A photographer from the *Tatler* had turned up to take my photograph because I had collaborated with my father and an uncle on a play which was now being performed at the Savoy Theatre and losing about

£5,000 a week. Since the car was standing in front of
the door he asked me to pretend to be doing something
to it. For instance, taking off the wheel nuts. I had
obliged him and forgotten to screw them up again.

'Cor!' exclaimed the A.A. man. 'Look at that! Best
part of 300 yard, I wouldn't wonder.'

He walked me back and sure enough a very neat
knife-like incision had been cut in the road for the
distance he wouldn't wonder. Years later, when the
war was over, and I visited Cambridge occasionally in
other cars, I always looked to see if that surgical scar
was still there. Until ten years ago it was. After seven-
teen years somebody had repaired the road.

I must tell you that my wife had lost her Austin
Seven. During our absence from home, my father had
given it to a cousin of mine who had gone to live with
him. This generous if immoral act meant that my wife
was largely housebound until weekends. So we decided
to make a tour of the second-hand establishments in
Cambridge. The yellow Renault, very much deteriorated, stood winter and summer under a tree in
my father-in-law's garden, with a coffee tin rigged up
to replace one of the hub caps. The stuffing was
coming out of the hood lining, the sandwich windscreen was blotched with blue and rust was devouring
it.

I persuaded my wife that it would be much cheaper
to buy a different car than have that thing made ready
for the road. And finally, after a great many trial
runs on rather boring Morris Tens and front-wheel-
drive Citroëns of the 'Maigret' variety, and other
residual mementos of the pre-war motoring days, we
settled on a rather attractive-looking Singer Ten.

I had had very little acquaintance with Singer cars,
except that I knew that they had once made an

extremely pretty little sports coupé. This one was a Ten saloon. I asked if I could drive it around the houses a bit and was immediately astounded. It had an overhead-camshaft engine which revved like the sewing machine of the same name, and when I gave a bit of a jab on the accelerator it shot away with about three times the acceleration of the Daimler. We bought it on the spot. I think it cost £130 and, except for some rather unpleasant noises in bottom gear it was sweet and true. Why use bottom gear anyway? I have never used bottom gear on any car I possessed.

And then the great day dawned.

I was sitting scribbling away at a desk in the good old *Sunday Chronicle*, when someone slapped down the latest edition at my elbow. I turned a rather bleary eye in his direction, and the words sprang from the page:

'SIX HUNDRED GALLONS OF
PETROL FOR ELECTION
CANDIDATES'

Six hundred gallons of p...! Could I have imagined it? No, there it was.

'SIX HUNDRED GALLONS OF
PETROL FOR ELECTION
CANDIDATES'

I didn't drive back to Cambridge that night. Instead I spent the night in town and, next morning, after looking up their address in the telephone book, I presented myself at the Liberal headquarters in Westminster.

They seemed quite glad to have me. There were rather more than 600 constituencies to fill, and the Liberals were determined to fight every one of them.

I asked if I could have a dormitory suburb. It seemed to me that my own rather peculiar personality would go down better in that sort of place than among

the shires, or the great industrial towns. I also wanted
to be able to get to it from Cambridge.

A very pleasant man said, 'How about Harrow
ast?'

Marvellous!' I exclaimed.

The good Liberal people of Harrow East seemed
quite glad to have me too, largely, I think, on account
of the petrol. It was part of the bargain that coupons
could be distributed among the owners of cars who
were prepared to offer them, full-time, to help the
candidate.

I made a lavish distribution of largesse, showing
great preference for cars with folding tops. I hired a
bevy of really beautiful girls and I wanted them to be
seen. I had a splendid pennant made, to fly from the
bonnet of the Daimler. In silver lettering on a blue
background it said, YOUR LIBERAL CANDIDATE.
Then I remembered the yellow Renault. That had a
folding top. So I got it sandpapered up a trifle, and,
with new plugs, a new battery and new tyres, it became capable of movement. That was a dreadful, in-
escapable car. It ran just as beautifully as it ever had.
I acquired a tall and Junoesque creature from the
A.T.S. to drive the Daimler. Apparently an election
overrode all else—even military duties. I persuaded
her to take off her ridiculous uniform and buy a
flowered Ascot hat. She really drove the Daimler very
well, being used to driving lorries and jeeps and
generals, except for a slight tendency to faint at the
wheel. The weather was inordinately hot, and the first
time she did this she was just able to pull in to the side
of the road before collapsing over the wheel. I soon
learned to detect the premonitory symptoms. One
finger would go up to sweep the hair out of the eyes.
Half a mile further on, her finger would go up again.

This was the time when I said, 'Better let me take over,'
and we would gratefully change places.

Soon I had about seven cars, all open, and all filled
with raging beauties.

I would lead the cavalcade, standing with a loud-
hailer in the back of the Daimler. At every worthwhile
street intersection I would stop the car and address the
multitude. From the cars behind the lovelies would
descend, making the very pavements to blossom, and
hand out leaflets.

It was fun while it lasted, but of course I didn't get
in. Secretly I have always been sorry about this. I
would have made a dedicated and idealistic member
of Parliament, and today I should really be gracing
the House of Lords.

So I went into publishing instead. Our offices were
in Beauchamp Place, just off the Brompton Road, and,
on the other side of the Brompton Road, in a place
called Cheval Place, lived Mr Paddon, who sold
second-hand, pre-war Rolls-Royces.

I must tell you about Mr Paddon. His proud claim
was that he was the man who had put the shutters on
the Rolls-Royce.

Every day at lunch time, my steps would unfalter-
ingly lead me across the road and under the archway,
to where the mews was littered with these exquisite
things, with their proud radiators, and their long lines,
each one an individual in its own right, with its own
personality, its own looks, and an aristocratic aura of
what I can only call breeding, of careful men bushing
little screws, lovingly polishing copper pipes, buffing
leather, rubbing down with cuttlefish bones, and
applying fourteen coats of paint.

One day, I could bear it no longer, and I entered in

like a man in trance.

There were no showrooms in the ordinary sense. Just a large shed, with two mechanics painstakingly working on one side, and about eight cars grouped about, waiting for attention, on the other. Some of them were really too early to be considered for ownership. There were several of the old 'Twenties' which in the twenties never did really more than parade the streets of London and Paris, in respectable silence. One of them had rather a pretty French body, with a French speedometer marked in kilometres. But I knew they had really no performance.

One of the prettiest pre-war Rollses, I always thought, was what was known as the Owen Sedanca de Ville.

I asked Captain Moore, who appeared to run the place, if he had any of these in the pipeline.

'No,' he said. 'But there's that.' And he pointed to the corner.

My eyes grew larger. The Owen Sedancas were made largely, I think, on the 'Twenty-Five' chassis. This one was a Phantom II, and was coachbuilt by Rippon. But it had the same sort of treatment. A square separate trunk at the rear with the spare wheel clamped to it, a cabriolet body, very reminiscent of coaching days, and a long bonnet, tapering to that blaze of silverware in front, with the famous lady, the Athenian radiator, the Paddon shutters, the lamps, the horns, the spotlamps, the bumpers, the overriders, the lot.

'I'd like to buy it,' I said, 'if we could agree on a price for my Daimler.'

He turned a rather beady eye on the Daimler.

'I think,' said Captain Moore, 'you ought to see Mr Paddon.'

'Ought I?'

113

'I'm sure this is something he'd like to handle
himself.'

'But I'm in town every day.'

'Could I ask where you live?'

'A place called Peaslake, in Surrey.'

'Oh, *well*! You're about four and a half miles from
him.'

'If you will tell me exactly how to get there?'

'I'll do that. And I'll tell you exactly how to behave
when you arrive.'

'Oh?' I said, slightly startled.

'Don't be surprised at anything that happens. And
the rules of the establishment are that not a word must
be said about motorcars until after tea.'

'Oh, I get tea!'

'You do,' Captain Moore said.

So the very next day, at about half past three in the
afternoon, after washing and leathering the Daimler
until it shone like silver, I motored over.

The place was a perfectly ordinary Surrey house of
the better sort, somewhere in the highlands south of
Dorking. It had a nice view, and there were roses
round the door. It was obviously Mrs Paddon, a grey-
haired lady, who answered my peal.

'Oh good afternoon,' said Mrs Paddon. 'Shall we go
straight in?'

She led me into a dining room, with a large square
Victorian table in the middle, covered with a cloth, and
set for four places. At the head of the table, in an
astonishing Victorian chair, high-backed and absurdly carved, sat an enormous yellow cat, surveying
the scene through half-closed eyes.

'Do sit down,' Mrs Paddon said, indicating the
chair opposite. She turned to the cat.

'Can I introduce Mr Gibbs?'

I could see the cat summing me up.

'How do you do!' I said, with becoming gravity.

'Mr Paddon will be in directly. Sit down. Sit down.'
She sat down herself, between me and the cat, and
began rattling teapots and cups. Then Mr Paddon
shambled in. He was an old man, in bedroom slippers,
which slipped and slopped on the threadbare carpet.

'Ah!' Mr Paddon exclaimed, shifting the pipe
from one hand to the other, so that we could shake. He
took the last remaining place.

'Has Mr Gibbs been properly introduced?'

'He has.'

'Good. Now we can talk. It's a bit eccentric, I know.
For what we are about to receive, may the Lord make
us truly thankful. How many Daimlers have you had?'

'This is my fourth, actually.'

He looked sympathetic.

'The great thing about the Rolls-Royce, Mr Gibbs,
is that the engine never gives the impression of turning
round. Bloody great pistons, in bloody great cylinders,
going slowly up and down, like bloody great lifts!'

I thought he was a splendid old man, and beamed at
him across a toasted teacake.

'These little cars—they can only be made to move at
all if the engine goes round and round like a mad
thing. Buzz-boxes! Now when you've got seven litres
of capacity, you can put in the same sort of gearing as
a bloody Pacific locomotive. My wife doesn't like me
saying "bloody".'

'I'm sorry to hear that.'

He gave me a sharp look.

'Are you making fun of me?'

'Good heavens, no!'

'Because if you are, Mr Chang won't like it.'

I hope my expression accepted the reproof.

'What someone's got to invent, one of these days, is
an engine that doesn't go round at all. The most
brilliant piece of engineering in thirty years was the
ramjet on the flying bomb. No moving parts at all!
Brilliant! The air just rushes in at the front, gets mixed
with paraffin, burns, and rushes out at the back.'

'What prevents it from rushing out at the front?'

'Just air pressure, my boy. Exactly the same principle as the ordinary blowtorch.'

'I know where you can buy them for fitting to
bicycles.'

The old boy's eyes lit up like blowtorches.

'Where?' he demanded.

'A shop in Cambridge. But that one does have a
valve in front, which flaps shut. Otherwise you'd have
to pedal at something like 300 mph before the engine
lit.'

He looked greedy.

'Will you buy me one?'

'Yes, if you'll make me a decent deal on the
Daimler.'

He nodded to his wife. She rose from the table,
after asking me if I was sure I didn't want another cup
of tea, went to the vast cat, bundled it under her arm,
and left the room with it.

At last, after the ceremonial had been duly attended
to, we went into the necessary rigmarole. He knew
which car I wanted, and asked an impossibly high
price for it. I said that was far too much.

'What you want then,' he said, 'is a little Bentley.'

I had never regarded the Bentley as particularly
'little'. I found the hauteur rather pleasing and said no,
I didn't want a little Bentley. I wanted a bloody great
Rolls, with bloody great pistons going up and down in
116 bloody great cylinders!

So at the end of it, we agreed a price, and he
promised to ring up Captain Moore. I got into the
Daimler, feeling rather repentant. I felt that it had been
belittled.

CHAPTER VIII

Of Rollses and Bentleys

I DON'T KNOW if you are familiar with the Phantom II?

The first thing you notice is the extreme difficulty of gaining the driver's seat. The gear lever and the brake lever are both on the right, just in front of where the door opens, and you have somehow to step over, round, or through these. Invariably, one of them goes up your trouser leg. If you are wearing an overcoat, one corner of this finds its way unhesitatingly into the open 'gate', so that when you move the gear lever you cut it, as with a pair of scissors. All three of my overcoats have torn places where this has happened.　119

I regard them as honourable scars, obtainable only by people accustomed to driving Rolls-Royces. The next thing you notice, when you start the engine, is that it sounds like a single-cylinder motor-bike—chug, chug, chug—the bloody great pistons et cetera. I remembered this from that Rolls we hired on the Riviera.

Then you start. You shove in second gear, to the sound of rending cloth. The clutch has rather a long travel. I should say it is something in the region of five inches, and to your astonishment you find that four of those inches cover the actual engagement. It is inexpressibly sweet. It is quite unnecessary to touch the accelerator. You simply slide the foot up and glide away. You are sitting, of course, rather high. This gives you a commanding sensation. You see over the tops of little cars. The eyes automatically focus for great distances. The next thing you notice is the air of intense respect accorded you. As you turn out of Cheval Place into the Brompton Road, the passing cars stop dead in their tracks, and their drivers wave you on. If a policeman is about to stop the traffic, he lets you through and *then* stops it. A modern Rolls still has shutters, but they are not Mr Paddon's sort of shutters. It was a very hot day when I accepted delivery of my Phantom, and I remember stopping somewhere in the Fulham Road to check the water level in the radiator. There was a girl attendant who came out with a large can. As she poured the cold water in, the shutters closed with a clang.

'Oo—er!' she said. 'What's that?'

They don't talk like that now. They don't make 'em like that either, as the saying goes.

There was a man on Putney Hill, occupying the centre of the road, in trouble with his gears. I walked past him on the inside. He was annoyed.

'Oi!' he yelled. 'Who gave *you* the Freedom of the Road?'

'Walked' is right. It is the entirely appropriate word. The Phantom did walk. There was a definite impression of footsteps. Long, lithe footsteps. Seven-league footsteps. I have no idea what the gear ratio was because there was no counter fitted. But on a later Rolls I found that at 60 mph the engine was turning over at 2,000. And once, when I drove it in France, and we touched 90 just to see, it was turning at 3,000, and the only sound was that wonderful high whine of the square-cut Dunlop tyres. They don't make *them* like that either. The last thing I remember of that triumphant journey was that the sun shone, the birds twittered in the trees, and my good friend, Mr Fincken, the Works Manager of a garage in Dorking, to whom I wanted to show off a little, put his bare forearm across his eyes as if to shield them from all that blazing chromium.

The way to our house is up a steep concrete road, with an incline of about one in six. The Rolls strode up it quietly in top gear. As I entered our own drive, all the cuckoos in Surrey were shouting.

My wife was standing on the steps of the house. She gave one look at it.

'What's its petrol consumption?' she asked.

There is a place in Brittany called Sables-d'Or-Les-Pins. It has three rather good hotels and the ruins of a casino, with shops all round, which was damaged by the Germans. The Rolls took us there, doing all of twelve miles to the gallon.

It should really have been doing ten, but the Rolls carburettor is very susceptible to fiddling. There are really two carburettors, the starting carburettor and another one for running. If you leave the starting carburettor alone, and unscrew the hexagon nut on the other, almost into the region of flat spots, you can actually get that extra two miles to the gallon. I have had fourteen in my time, but that entailed a certain amount of juggling with the right foot to catch the engine before it died.

The French thought nothing of the Rolls. They shrugged their shoulders at its vast size. Its shape meant nothing to them.

'*C'est ancienne*,' they said.

The French lost two things in the war. One was their soul. The other was their taste. The citizens of the country of Chapron and Figoni were now perfectly content to drive around in some of the most repulsive motorcars that it has been my lot to behold.

Can anybody conceive any lines more nauseating than those conferred upon the original two-cylinder Citroën? They can. Easily. The Citroën Ami trundles all over France, carrying fat men with fierce mustachios, looking like the Tea House of the August Moon. If the ancient Egyptians, 5,000 years ago, with their well-known affection for the Lotus, had produced a chariot of this shape, they might have been forgiven.

I am led to mention this, because in order to avoid the main beach, which was cluttered with the same people one saw at meals, I followed one of those grotesque machines, containing a pleasant French family in bathing suits, to see where it went.

It went past the three hotels, along the village street, past the dance hall on the left which resounded nightly with the riot of the Samba, and then made a right-hand turn, which took it down a leafy lane which led, after three monumental bumps, directly on to the sand. Lurching

horribly, the pagoda-like object continued unchecked.

The Brittany tides, as you probably know, ebb and flow, literally, for miles. At nearby Mont St Michel, which is not in Brittany but in Normandy, the tide recedes for a full six miles. It comes in, so they say, with the speed of a galloping horse.

The tide was out now, but it had left lagoons behind it. The surface seemed firm enough, so we urged the Rolls gently forward. As we did so, twenty or thirty waiters from the hotels who had submerged themselves in one of the lagoons at the sight of the Citroën, stood up naked. Then they saw the Rolls. I never witnessed a quicker full-knees-bend. The Citroën, it now became clear, was heading for a distant promontory. It had a lighthouse on it, and some kind of tower or fort. We didn't want to follow the contraption too closely out of politeness, so we let them get ahead by 300 or 400 yards. On the other hand, we thought they probably knew where the track was firmest, and where the lagoons were, whether or not furnished with naked waiters. So we kept to a very imitative course.

Ten minutes later, they were climbing among sand dunes, lurching like a small boat in a rough sea. When we arrived at the same place I jibbed a little at putting two and a half tons of Rolls-Royce into such a situation, but we did seem to have reached the point of no return, and presently, with spinning wheels, and highly untenable angles, we came across other cars on firm ground.

There was the little castle. There was the lighthouse, and there, below us, was an enchanting little harbour, with a charming harbour wall. And what's more, there was deep water in it.

I like bathing from harbour walls. There is generally nice hot brick or concrete on which to sit. You can dive in without that chilly walk and, when you've had

enough, you climb up some steps, and spread your
wetness on the hot concrete again.

So we disported ourselves.

But not for long. If there was water in the harbour
there would soon be water between the headland and
the hotels in Sables-d'Or. It was possible, some other
people said, to drive round by Erquy on a proper road,
but that was all of ten kilometres round. So when there
was a scurry to get back across the beach, we joined
in the exodus, and a whole covey of cars plunged
across, sometimes on dry sand, sometimes in about
three inches of water.

We made it all right. But when we arrived at our
hotel, outside which a lot of people were sitting at
tables and chairs stretching halfway across the road,
the Rolls sidled up to them at a speed intended to
create an impression of stately approach. At exactly
the right moment, I applied the footbrake, and exactly
nothing happened. I realized that we were about to
slice through those happy aperitif drinkers, like
Boadicea's chariot. The drinkers seemed to realize it
almost as quickly. They exploded into a kaleidoscopic
sunburst of men, women, and children, most of whom
seemed to want to take a chair or bottle with them as
they fled. Fortunately the handbrake worked. We stopped, nudging the nearest table on two of its four legs.

'I'm terribly sorry, everybody!' I said. 'I've got
absolutely no brakes.'

The French vociferated and shook their fists.

'My God, old man!' said an English voice.

'*Assassin!*' cried a French one.

'I'm frightfully sorry, but I haven't got any brakes at
all!'

'Well you'd better do something to quell the mob. I
think that chap over there's about to lynch you.'

'Well what do I do?'

'Drinks all round, old man, I suppose.'

I rose in the front seat, and cried in a loud voice, '*Le même pour tous.*'

The waiter nodded and bustled away.

The effect was magical. Very slowly, so as not to give an inkling of too instant conversion, and in a chorus of grumbling on all sides, the people resumed their places. Five waiters appeared with trays laden with sparkling glasses.

'Cost you a pretty penny, old man,' the Englishman said.

I backed the car about ten feet away, and the Gibbs family advanced. We seated ourselves at the nearest table, now on its four legs again.

The man who had been about to lynch me suddenly lifted a milky Pernod in my direction.

'*Vive l'Angleterre!*' he shouted.

'*Vive la France!*' I shouted back.

Harmony was restored.

The Englishman at the next table tilted his chair back so that we could address each other diagonally.

'What do you mean, you haven't got any brakes?'

'I haven't got any brakes!'

'Some oversight at Derby?'

'Driving about in the sea, I suppose.'

He shook his head.

'You shouldn't do things like that, old man. Not in a nice car. They'll dry out.'

'You think so?'

'Absolutely certain sure. Can I buy you a drink?'

But they didn't. The next morning there were still no brakes. And the morning after that, there were still no brakes. It wasn't water which had got into them. It was sand.

Somehow I didn't relish the idea of the local improviser taking apart those brakes. An Austin Swallow,
yes. A Rolls-Royce, no. I felt it necessary that Albert
should work on them, in Cheval Place. So for ten
days, I drove that car up and down the road to the
little headland via Erquy on the handbrake alone.
In some ways that Erquy detour was the making of
our holiday, because we could go round when the tide
was high and all the other lunatics had left us the
place for ourselves.

On the last day we had to drive to Dieppe, in order
to catch the ferry to Newhaven. Dieppe was all of
200 miles. Driving 200 miles on the handbrake is
hard work, I can assure you. The hardest part was not
putting the brake on, as you might imagine, but
squeezing the ratchet lever to take it off again. I had
looked out on the map an alternative route which
avoided the traffic of the main roads. I thought to
myself that if we did our motoring more or less by
ourselves, it would be considerably less nerve-
wracking than doing crash stops in heavy traffic. I was
right about this, but unfortunately, at about the halfway mark, we had to cross a large river. I imagine it
was the Seine. I naturally expected that we should be
supplied with a bridge. Not so. Instead there was a
plunging little ferry tootling back and forth, and
carrying about six cars on every journey. Somehow or
other, we had to get our beast first down a steep ramp,
then across a bobbling wooden gangplank that shifted
continuously, and then into a position on deck which
allowed access to other cars. I remembered that I had
a friend once who went over the edge when coming
back from that island, on which I dimly remember a
casino, somewhere in the region of Hampton Court.
He drowned his wife. We could all swim fairly

126

competently, but I was nervous about the car.

Finally, inspiration descended. The thing was to leave the handbrake firmly fixed in the 'on' position and use the power of the engine to overcome its resistance. We not only got on board the vessel safely, but we backed up to within inches of an extremely fragile rail, overlooking the water. There was a formidable smell of burnt linings, and quite a quantity of smoke, which everybody was kind enough to point out.

The other side was dead easy. We simply took off for dry land.

At Dieppe, they still winched cars aboard, by crane. And the same thing happened at Newhaven. As we stood and watched this tremulous operation, the feeling came to me that the Rolls had taken a dislike for the continent of Europe, and would agree to allow us to use its brakes the moment it was on English soil.

While we waited our turn at the Customs, I remembered that the old Phantom IIs had a pedal which delivered oil to all the joints. Such a good idea! I gave about thirty pumps to this pedal, moved six inches, and applied the brakes. They worked immediately.

I regret to report that my wife seized the opportunity provided by the brake failure to start begging me in real earnest to get rid of the car.

I was commuting five or six days a week to my publishing business in London, and was eating up petrol at the rate of seven gallons for every journey. Added to this, instead of the flat-rate tax of £25 for every vehicle on the road of whatever size, we were in those days paying £1 for every Royal Automobile Club horsepower. I am not sure that during this period the tax did not rise to thirty shillings. Since the R.A.C.

rating was forty-five, this meant that in one case I was
paying £45 annually, and in the other, if my arithmetic
isn't faulty, £67 10s. Secretly, I rather agreed with her
about all this. It *was* rather a majestic mode of travel
in the circumstances.

The great thing about Rolls-Royces is that they
never wear out. Therefore they do not depreciate, to
any noticeable extent. Nowadays, of course, those
machines of the thirties are selling at exactly the same
prices that they fetched in the forties. A superb
example, with a really elegant body, in good shape,
will now fetch five times the forties price.

I didn't know that then. But once bitten by the
Rolls-Royce bug, it is not easy to disinfect the system.
I decided to search the advertising columns for a
Twenty-Five.

I found one almost at once, in a mews off Exhibition
Road in London. It was, of course, a much smaller
car, but the same craftsmanship was there. The engine
of the Twenty-Five was a much later design than that
of the Phantom, and it was used, suitably hotted up,
for the new Rolls-Bentley, once advertised as 'The
Silent Sports Car'. This one was a four-seater drophead, and its lines, I thought, were more refined.

We went for a drive around the park, and, although
the giant strides were missing, it travelled with neat-
ness, quietness and precision. The man assured me
that I should get a good twenty miles to the gallon.
The tax was less than half what I was paying on the
Phantom, and finally the prospect of domestic bliss
persuaded me. I drove home in it.

I can only suppose that the Rolls people up in
Derby were acting on a deliberate policy. Here was
practically the same chassis with, basically, the same
128 engine as the Bentley which was perfectly happy at

speeds of 90 and more mph, and yet the absolute maximum built into this machine was of the order of 65 mph. Only once, by brutally thrashing it downhill, did I succeed in pushing it up to 70. I would still very much like to know what it was they did to that engine to prevent it going at what was now becoming the common speed of traffic.

Road speeds have, of course, risen dramatically as the years roll by. It's a question of the common car. In the days of my white Salmson, which would just nudge the mile-a-minute mark, most people drove at a steady 35 mph, with an occasional burst of 40. In the forties, most of the common cars could maintain a steady 50 for hours on end and most of them did. Today, I find that if I maintain a steady mile-a-minute in the middle lane of a three-lane dual carriageway there is a constant 'Wuff . . . Wuff . . . Wuff' as every car on the road, Minis, Hillman Imps, Morris Minors, Vauxhalls, Fords, and even unladen lorries, goes rushing past my right ear.

I don't find this dangerous in any way. I find it bad for discipline. And when my Twenty-Five was hounded from behind by some beastly Javelin, or treated with disrespect by two-stroke motorcycles and young louts with funny hats, it did seem to me an insult to the memory of the Hon. Charlie Rolls and the dedicated Mr Royce.

What I do find dangerous, if I might be allowed to continue this monologue for a paragraph or two, is the modern habit of driving by the white line. My mother used to hear her Arthur say, "Ug the corners and 'oot like 'ell!' My own first rule of motoring has consistently been 'Always be able to stop in the distance ahead you can see to be clear'. The modern generation completely ignores this first principle and

129

has developed a new technique, which scares the living
daylights out of me.

The system, applied lavishly in the twisting lanes
near to where I live, is simply that, if you keep within
the white line, you can go round blind corners as fast
as you like.

This system works tolerably well if you are driving,
say, a Mini, so long as the other fellow is also driving
a Mini. But supposing he isn't? Suppose he's driving
a ten-ton lorry? Or there's a woman with a perambula-
tor? Or simply someone going to post a letter at the
confluence of two Minis? And what happens then?
The squeal of tyres, and a head-on crash.

The extraordinary thing is that the white-line
drivers, and even officialdom, seem to regard the head-
on crash as a perfectly normal concomitant of getting
about. Fit seat belts. Wear seat belts. Have padded
facias. Build windscreens so that you can go through
them safely. Make steering columns easy to fracture,
so that they don't stab you in the throat. Box-weld a
'safety cage' so the engine won't come into the car.
Fit headrests to prevent your neck being broken on
impact. Fix balloons all over the place which blow
themselves up if heavily shaken.

I mustn't run ahead of events. The Twenty-Five
conducted me graciously every day from Peaslake to
Beauchamp Place, with effortless distinction, so long
as I travelled within the prescribed rules.

When we first had offices in Beauchamp Place it was
still possible to park outside the building. But this
didn't last long. All you had to do was to turn the
corner into Lennox Gardens, and there you might or
might not find three cars standing beside the railings.
Today, there are three thousand and three. One of the
three, a black Austin, arrived daily a few seconds before

I did, and out of it would step Roberta. Do you remember Roberta? It was that fighter-pilot and racing
motorist who turned into a lady. And a very pretty
one too, with long fair hair, curled at the tips where it
fell on the shoulders, and a very neatly tailored dark
suit. There was a click of high heels, and she was gone.

The small Rolls seemed to carry more chromium
plate at the front end than its predecessor. I believe it
was a 1937 model, and this meant that it had two
exposed trumpet horns carried on the dumb irons, and
a hooded spotlamp mounted centrally between them.

I mention this because I had an accident. Had I
been writing this before last Sunday, I could have
said that it was the only accident I ever had in all my
career of crashing about the roads. Last Sunday I did
precisely the same thing, twenty years later. Obviously it is a habit of which I must rid myself.

It is an easy situation to explain but not to justify.
In Dorking, there is a handy little back road which
cuts out all the traffic of the High Street, and brings
one out into the fast dual carriageway of the By-pass.

Usually, there is a little queue of waiting cars, their
drivers peering anxiously for gaps in the traffic.

Generally, they emerge into the main stream one by
one, and the rest of the line, patiently waiting its turn,
moves up into station. After a minute or two of this,
only a large empty lorry with its tailgate down stood
between me and heady freedom. I could see the driver's
head, through a square hole cut out in the back of his
cab. It was swinging round anxiously from side to side.
Then something about the angle of his ears flashed the
message that he was about to move forwards. He did
so. Now it was my turn to concentrate on the rush of
traffic. I stuck my head out of the side-window and
engaged second gear, all ready for a surge forward

when the moment came. There is supposed to be a
30 mph limit at that spot, but the traffic came surging
past at never less than 50 mph. Far to the right I
could see the breakthrough coming and kept my eye
on it, with my right foot poised. Here it came! I
jabbed the accelerator, banged in the clutch, and
crashed straight into the tail gate of the lorry, which
was still standing in front of me, quietly at rest. There
was an almighty noise of impact, followed by a
tinkling shower of glass that seemed to continue for
several minutes. The lorry driver's head almost came
through the square hole behind him. He banged his
nape on the bottom half of it. It must have hurt him.

With a feeling of nausea, I got out to inspect the
damage, while the lorry driver quietly drove away. I
suppose he was anxious not to get his employers
involved in an insurance dispute.

The chaos was appalling. The beautiful Lucas
P. 100s were smashed to smithereens. The horns were
twisted absurdly. So were Mr Paddon's shutters. And
the fan was making nasty knocking noises against the
back of the radiator, from which water steamed like a
pissing horse.

The only thing to do was to cross the road by the
underpass, enter the station, and buy myself a ticket
to London. Obviously, I had to consult Mr Paddon.

'What you need,' Mr Paddon said, as he had said
once before, 'is a nice little Bentley.'

I did not know then that Bentleys were inclined to
bring me bad luck and I was prepared to consider the
idea.

As luck would have it, there stood, in the small
assembly of cars waiting attention, a 1936 three-and-a-
half-litre, with all its paint stripped down to the
132 aluminium. One of the most beautiful fastbacks that

I had ever seen, by Gurney Nutting. You could tell
the thirty-sixes, because their horns had not yet
sprouted trumpets, and had flat faces which beeped
in a high-pitched chord. If an impression of speed is
what you're looking for, the Bentley radiator, with a
fastback tailing away behind it, is, in that sort of way,
more satisfactory than the Rolls. I realized that I
would have to alter my character completely if I was
to drive it. This was definitely a sporting machine,
which had the most engaging outward curve along the
bottom of its body rather like Roberta's curls. The
clinching argument was that, since it was unpainted, I
could specify any colour I liked.

Without a moment's hesitation I said, 'Metallic
grey, with a thin red line.'

Mr Paddon clapped his hands. Captain Moore's
eyes lit up. Even Albert, who was very deaf, and didn't
hear generally what people were saying, picked that
one up and looked ecstatic.

And so it was. While waiting for the paintwork and
the cuttlefish bones to be applied, I found in an
accessory shop a most amusing lamp. You mounted
it in the usual Rolls-Bentley position, at the foot of the
radiator, but its speciality was that its innards were
connected by cable to a lever on the steering column.
As you moved this lever, upwards, downwards, sideways, or in any direction you liked, so the reflector of
the lamp moved, so delicately that with its pencil
beam you could write letters on the oncoming scenery.
Later on, I found this to be one of the most useful
gadgets ever invented. In the fast lane, for instance, of
a dual carriageway you could position it straight ahead
and pointing slightly downwards, so that you got a
perfect view forwards without a glimmer of light
penetrating the back windows of the cars you were

passing. It also gave warning of your approach. In fog, you could wave it from side to side to get a glimpse of both verges of the road. In that awkward position which causes so much dazzle, when a road dips slightly to the left so that your dipped headlamps shine directly into the eyes of oncoming drivers, you could point it even further to the left or tip it further down, so that you could still see, and cause them no inconvenience whatsoever.

If I remember correctly, it took about three weeks before the car was due for delivery. In the meantime a friend of mine, who published one or two of my books, was decent enough to lend me what he called his cottage, on the Isle of Wight. It was in Bembridge, which is generally considered rather the smart part of the island, on account of its expensive connection with yachting.

I hadn't been on the Isle of Wight since I went there with the Monocar, and it was amusing to revive old memories of the ferryboats. When we got to Bembridge, it took a certain amount of asking in the shops to find Rose Cottage.

I wouldn't have called it a cottage myself. It was a charming little Georgian house. Next door to it was an exactly similar little Georgian house, separated from the other by a hedge. The two short driveways had gates approximately three feet apart, and, as we drove up, at precisely the same moment our former Rolls, which I had left unbefriended in Dorking, crept up the other drive, so that we arrived together at our respective front doors, absolutely simultaneously to the second.

I was so excited and astounded by this remarkable coincidence, that I rushed through a gap in the hedge, shouting, 'That's my car! That's my car.'

134

The people in the car regarded me with the gravest suspicion.

'What do you mean, it's your car?'

'It's my car,' I shouted. 'That's my car you're in!' The driver descended, with a look in his eye which appeared to mean that he was ready to meet trouble with trouble.

'I'm extremely sorry to have to inform you,' he said, 'that it's *my* car. I accepted delivery of it only this morning.'

'That's right,' I said. 'You bought it from Paddon's, didn't you? 60 Cheval Place. I sold it to them only the other day! Isn't that the most amazing coincidence?'

He was quite unmollified. He was also struck dumb. Not with astonishment, but at dislike of my crude behaviour.

'Look in the log book, man,' I cried, 'if you don't believe me! My name is Gibbs. Anthony Gibbs.'

'I really don't see that this is of any particular interest. Or any business of yours.'

I looked at the lamps and the horns and the radiator. They were unmarked—as good as new.

'Oh well—' I said. 'Sorry and all that.'

He watched me retreat in the gap in the hedge. We didn't speak to each other again.

It's a nice little place, Bembridge. But chilly. There always seems to be a North wind, which rustles the leaves of the poplars. If you want to find a place where it is warm enough to bathe, you have to drive along the South coast, along something called 'The Military Road' where there are gaps in the red cliffs, and where you can scramble down to a beach, suitably protected from the North.

The road is very straight. Since there is a Roman

135

villa at one end of it, I suspect it of being a Roman road. At night an occasional bus travels along it, but in those days there was very little traffic. Today there is a bonnet-to-tail procession of would-be nudists, I understand.

One night, driving the family home, exhausted, but singing after our exertions, I was, without realizing it, idly waving the pencil beam from side to side in time with the music. In the distance, half a mile away, was a bus coming in our direction. The family modulated into 'Smoke gets in your eyes', and I went on marking time with the beam. The bus flashed its headlights. I didn't really notice. What I did notice was that the bus was itself weaving from side to side, also in time with the music, until finally it pulled off the road altogether and came to a stop, brushing the hedge.

We carried on, unthinking.

It was only afterwards, with a shock of dismay, that I realized the bus driver thought he was confronted, not with a weaving light, but by some madman in a weaving car.

I still didn't know that Bentleys brought me bad luck. But that was a delicious car. It had all the solidity and the workmanship of the Rolls-Royce. Even the nuts on the engine shone like new. It was obviously built to last for ever. But, added to those excellencies, it was sweet and silent, right to the upper limits, which I never attempted. At 85 mph it swept forwards with a soundless rush. When it stood still people looked at it with pleasure. I remember a lorry driver, who drew up beside me on Chelsea Bridge.

'1936?' he asked.

When you opened the bonnet, the engine, to my untutored eye, was exactly the same as on the Twenty-Five Rolls. Why then did the engineers build so much litheness into that graceful car while its elder sister was deliberately limited to a maximum of 65 mph? I can only suppose it was to avoid the taint of 'Badge Engineering'. But 'Badge Engineering' is now almost universal. There is now no difference whatever between the Rolls-Royce and the Bentley, except that one is slightly more expensive and looks rather more like a Peugeot than the other.

The people at my office were so pleased with my little Bentley, that they used to make me take them for little tootles round the park, after lunch, just to freshen us up for the afternoon. But I told you it brought me bad luck.

The trouble was simple enough. It might have happened to anyone. Unfortunately, it happened to me, because I was the principal shareholder in a quite successful little firm called Allan Wingate Ltd.

One day, a strike in the printing industry was called. At all events the owners described it as a strike. But the strikers themselves called it a lock-out. Whatever it was, the results were exactly the same.

We had two best-sellers on our hands. One was a book called *Exodus* by an American writer, Leon Uris, and the other was a book entitled *The Desert Generals* by Corelli Barnett. We had actually sold 9,000 copies of Bill Barnett's book before we even published it, and *Exodus* had actually clocked up 20,000 copies, which we regarded as a fantastic pre-publication subscription, as it's called.

The books were printed and bound, and actually sitting in the warehouse of the printer, down at Exeter. In most cases, a book sells approximately three times after publication what it sells before, so that we could reasonably count on 60,000 copies of *Exodus* and 30,000 of *The Generals*. Since our profit on the sale of

a book of this sort used to be exactly £1, we had a
pleasant feeling in the pits of our stomachs that
£90,000 was coming our way. Apart from that slightly
heady prospect, we knew we had just under £30,000
in the kitty the moment the books were delivered.

The printers were unable to deliver the books.

I pleaded with them. I cajoled them. I telephoned
three times daily. I offered to go down myself, heading
a fleet of lorries, and to make a speech to the pickets. I
got in touch with the Master Printer's Association.

I don't want to build up too big a story over this, but
I do in my mind definitely connect it with the Bentley,
as you will see if you read on.

The strike lingered on for two months. The trouble
with not getting in any money for two months is that all
the people you owe money to expect to be paid just as
if nothing were happening. In a very short time indeed
we couldn't pay anybody anything. Publishing is as
hand-to-mouth an operation as that. We had a man
from the Gas Board sitting all day in one of our chairs.
Those particular printers couldn't very well ask us
for our money before they handed over the books, but
there were lots of other printers, who had handed over
books before the strike began, and they expected to
be paid. The whole thing snowballed in a terrifying
fashion. So we called a Creditors' Meeting.

I drove up to it in the Bentley.

There used to be a place opposite the K.L.G.
factory near the Robin Hood Gate of Richmond Park,
where you could turn left and go up a smallish road,
which brought you out on to the top of Putney Hill.

I turned into this, and found that about two-thirds
of the road was poled off, with red hurricane lamps
hanging at the corners. A man came climbing over one
of the poles and pointed very authoritatively at the

ground just in front of the car. This clearly meant
stop. So I stopped. To my astonishment, the man
opened the door and climbed in.

'That's very kind of you, sir,' he said.

I cried out. 'Am I supposed to be giving you a lift?'

'That's right, sir. Very kind of you.'

'How do you know I want to give you a lift?'

'Because you stopped, sir. And I got in.'

'Damn it. You came out of the road works as if you
were some sort of County Council Inspector or something.'

'That's right, sir. It's a good one. They always stop.
I'm a professional beggar.'

'Well I'll be damned.'

'That's right, sir. I stops them at a road works, and
ask them where they are going, so I know how much
time I've got to soften them up. May I ask where are
you going, sir?'

'Can you soften me up before Beauchamp Place?'

'I'll do my best, sir.'

'Then *I'll* tell *you* a story. I've got a majority holding
in a publishing firm called Allan Wingate. We've got
two books. One's called *Exodus* by an American chap,
Leon Uris, and the other's called *The Desert Generals*
by my friend Bill Barnett.'

'Is that so, sir?'

'Yes. The moment I can get my hands on those
books, I can get my hands on £30,000. But I can't get
the ruddy things, because there's been a ruddy
printers' strike for two ruddy months. So I'm on my
way to a Creditors' Meeting, at which we will undoubtedly go bust.'

All the way through Putney and along the King's
Road I told him the story.

'How much are you going to go bust for, sir?'

'D'you mean me, personally?'

'Yes, sir.'

'About £18,000.'

His voice was reverential.

'I wish I could help you, sir.'

'So do I.'

We arrived at Number 12, Beauchamp Place in silence, and I reached across him to open the door.

He got out.

'Thanks', he said, 'for the buggy-ride.'

I watched him go. Then we both saw the same thing. There were road works of no mean dimensions, bringing riot and confusion to the Brompton Road.

He turned, took off his cap, and gave me a sweeping bow. Then he held up a little zero, made of his thumb and first finger. I knew what that meant. It meant Good Luck to both of us.

We went bust all right. And I lost my £18,000 which, apart from this house, was pretty well all I had.

Going home that evening, along the King's Road, and feeling sick at heart, I suddenly realized that without seeing it, I had been travelling behind the most beautiful car I have ever seen. It was a big black Rolls, shaped very much as my old Delage, but more beautiful still, because, instead of being a drophead, it had a marvellously square-cut top like a brougham.

I can't think what came over me. I suppose it was the backlash from the Creditors' Meeting.

I drew up beside him when the lights stopped and shouted across.

'Excuse me,' I said, 'but will you sell me your car?'

'Certainly,' he said. 'It's for sale.'

I could have beaten my chest with exultation.

The lights turned green.

'Are you the owner?'

'No, I'm taking it down to Roehampton to show a customer.'

Every motor horn in the King's Road began to blare at once.

'Well don't show it to him. I'll buy it.'

'Well, who are you?'

I told him.

'Well, how do I find you?'

The lights turned red.

'Do you know Paddon's?'

'Of course.'

'I'll meet you there tomorrow morning at eleven o'clock, chequebook in hand.'

He saluted.

The lights turned green.

I watched him make a left-hand turn, waved a hand in case he could see it in his mirror, and went on my way straight ahead, singing at the top of my voice.

'Well?' my wife said.

'Wound up,' I told her. 'And I've sold the Bentley.'

'Sackcloth and ashes?'

'In a way. It rather looks as though I'd bought a Rolls.'

I presented myself at Paddon's the next morning a quarter of an hour too early. I had meant to explain to them what was happening and ask them to help me in the little matter of price. But the car was already there, with an admiring group walking round it. They parted to let me through.

'We know this car,' Captain Moore said. 'It's been through our hands. 1933 Phantom II Continental. Body by Freestone and Webb.'

Standing well back, I thought it was the loveliest thing I had ever seen, and I still think so. Its shape was extraordinarily similar to that of my Delage. The

same massive prow. The same small body, sitting
about halfway back. The same helmet wings. The
same gigantic headlights. Its proportions were so
perfect that it looked like a two-seater. I have carried
a photograph of it about ever since. Yet there was
room on that back seat for three people, with their
legs stretched right out in front of them.

'A gentleman's carriage,' said Captain Moore.

There was one slight flaw in perspective, I thought.
From the back, the boot, instead of following the
straight line from the radiator, as in the case of the
Delage, tapered in; but it had, of course, a great fat
wheel with a great fat tyre, stuck on behind, which
hid the blemish. I decided that perhaps a fattish
bumper would make it seem to sit more squarely on
the road. And it didn't have a lady on the bonnet.
They had plenty of those. The door was politely
opened for me, and the gear lever went up my trouser
leg. It was marvellous to have once again that sensation
of sitting well inside a car, instead of on it. Only one's
head showed in the window. That was the high-
waisted look like Josephine. The last thing I want to
see when driving about is the road rushing under
one's front wheels, and the kerbs flashing by on either
side.

My wife has a Mini. I find it not only exhausting to
be perched up to watch all this countryside hurtling
by, but terrifying as well. If she drives me at more
than forty miles an hour in that thing, I grind my teeth;
and if the suspension works, I travel with one hand on
the roof.

The Rolls was not a bit like that. The view from the
driving seat was distant, in all directions. In front, the
majestic bonnet and radiator prevented the sight of
anything much nearer than twenty yards. On either

hand, you could see no child under eight or nine. The
window in the back was minuscule, and at least this
prevented the man behind seeing the set of one's ears.
All Ford Anglias should have this feature.

Naturally, there were occasional disadvantages. But
before I tell you the story of how I ran over an old
gentleman on a zebra crossing, I must explain to you
how the front seats, in order to avoid that trousering
business, had a most splendid and intricate little
arrangement. You could set the seat semi-permanently
in the position you liked most, lock it there, and then if
you wanted to get out there was another little catch
down between the legs which allowed the seat to slide
quite far back, so that you could then clamber ashore
gracefully, *behind* those two levers. When you wished
to enter the motorcar again, the seat was waiting for
you, and when you had sat in it, you simply rolled
forward until it clicked into its original position. I
don't know whether it was Mr Freestone or Mr Webb
who conceived of this, but it was well done.

To come straight to the point, this bizarre incident
occurred after I had driven myself away from Paddon's
glowing with pride and pleasure in the astonishing
fact that not only had I not had to sign a cheque for my
new acquisition; I had actually received a small sum
of money for the exchange.

Perhaps it was this which numbed the brain. I had
been for a little circle round the park to get the feel
of the car, and was now zigzagging about in residential
streets, with some idea of filling in the time pleasantly
before a lunch date with a well-known spy.

I don't know if you remember Eddie Chapman? He
was that astonishing character who pretended to the
Germans that he was prepared to spy for them, and
was parachuted into England, with instructions to

143

blow up the De Havilland factory on the Barnet By-
pass.

They got the camouflage boys on to the thing, and
they went to work, simulating a vast area of destruc-
tion. A German plane was then allowed in to photograph the result and, a few weeks later, Eddie was
ferried to Lisbon in a British submarine, reported to
the German Embassy, and received the Iron Cross.

I cannot remember now exactly in what part of
London I was when this thing occurred, but, as I
turned out of those village high streets which are such
a feature of London, I noticed a motorcycle cop,
seated astride his machine, keeping his eye open for
possible victims. About a hundred yards further on,
I noticed a largish church with a great many tomb-
stones.

Suddenly a woman screamed. I think this is the only
time in my life I ever heard a woman scream. It was a
very loud and unpleasing noise. The next moment I saw
a hand coming upwards to clutch the lady on the top
of the radiator. I instinctively jammed my right foot
hard on the brake. At that moment, the seat unlatched
itself and rolled back about fifteen inches, so that I had
practically to lie down in order to stop the car.

The brain works very quickly on these occasions,
and an awful lot of things seem to be able to happen in
half a second of time. When I clambered out, dithering
in every limb, I found that the front of the car was
only *just* over the beginning of a Zebra crossing, and a
charming old gentleman was down on one knee.

I don't think he was hurt at all. When he had seen
that the car was cruising up to him, and was not,
apparently, going to stop, *his* instinct was to put up his
hands to stop it. I was profuse in my apologies, and
144   helped him to his feet, and dusted him off. Suddenly

the air was filled with a loud motorcycle clatter, and the cop arrived, with his pencil and notebook in his teeth. He called everybody 'sir'.

'How did this happen, sir? Failing to stop at a pedestrian crossing is a very serious offence indeed, sir. Are you injured in any way, sir? Do you propose to make a claim?'

So we had to go through with it. It was that bloody woman's scream. The chap had heard it from a hundred yards away.

'I'm all right, officer,' the old gentleman said. 'I'm perfectly all right. Fortunately the car did stop in time. Bit of a shock, that's all.' He was panting.

'I strongly advise you to see a doctor, sir.' He switched something on and started talking into his walkie-talkie.

'No, really!' the old gentleman said.

'I'm afraid I must insist, sir.' And in what seemed no time at all a white ambulance cruised up, and the old gentleman, protesting violently, was heaved gently aboard by willing hands, and departed from my life.

It was my turn.

'The seat slid,' I said stupidly.

'What do you mean, sir, the seat slid?'

'The seat slid,' I repeated.

'But that's a beautiful Rolls-Royce, sir. The seats don't slide, unless you want them to.'

'This one did,' I said.

I didn't tell the cop that the man had been completely invisible to me until I saw his hand. I opened the door, and showed him how the seat worked. 'It's the first time I've driven it. I suppose I hadn't got it latched properly.'

The cop examined the mechanism.

'Seems highly insecure to me, sir. Well I'm afraid

145

I'll have to take full particulars. Name and address,
please! Driving licence, please. Insurance certificate,
please.'

Still trembling, I produced the information and
particulars.

He wrote it all down.

'I'm afraid I shall have to book you, sir. You'll be
hearing from the magistrate in due course.'

I thanked him, weakly.

He watched me get into the car, move the seat
forward, till it was tethered, with an audible click.
Then he wheeled away. I was free to go.

I told Eddie Chapman about the experience, at
lunch. Eddie was amazed.

'Didn't you tip him?' he demanded.

'Tip him?'

'Damn it. Every sensible motorist carries a five-
pound note, mistakenly slipped into his driving
licence.'

'Good heavens!'

'You must act immediately. They could put you
away for that. You'll have to tip higher up, that's all.'

'Tip higher up? Tip whom?'

'Station superintendent, I should think. What area
of London was it?'

I told him. I was only pretending when I said I
didn't know. 'How much?'

'Twenty quid.'

'Good God! You mean to tell me I walk into the
station, ask to see the station superintendent, and slip
him twenty quid?'

'Of course!'

'But I can't do that.'

'All right then. I'll do it for you! Have you got
146 twenty quid?'

'Not unless he'll take a cheque.'

'Don't be an ass. They'll cash one for you here.'

The head waiter was summoned.

'Certainly, Monsieur.'

I wrote out a cash cheque for £20 and handed it to him. The money came on a silver salver. I indicated Eddie. Somehow I felt I ought not even to touch the stuff. Eddie took the money and stuffed it in his pocket.

'O.K. We'd better go. Can you give me a lift?'

'I'm not going near that place.'

'Extraordinary man! All right, I'll take a taxi.'

He went off. I made my way to the Rolls. I noticed that one of its headlights was slightly askew. I managed to put it straight. Then I made my way to the office.

It was at about quarter to three, when the telephone girl came through. 'There's a gentleman here,' she said, 'asking for Tony.'

'Does that mean me?'

'There aren't any others.'

'Did you ask him who he was?'

'He won't say. He just says he wants to speak to Tony.'

I didn't connect the thing in my mind.

'All right, put him through.'

'Is that Tony?'

'Yes. It is.'

'Oh. Well I just wanted to thank you. That'll be all right.'

'Oh good.'

'The only thing is, old fella—'

'Yes?'

'Don't do it again, old boy. That's all.'

There was a click.

The good Lord only knows what the effect on my   147

wife would have been, if I had not made that un-
expected £100 on the Bentley.

That happy event enabled me to keep the car for
five years. When my wife, joined later by my father,
cross-questioned me about petrol consumption, and
accused me of giving the wrong impression, I was
always able to say, 'After all, I did make a hundred
quid on it.' And for five years, that partially satisfied
them.

After that one unfortunate incident on the zebra
crossing, the car and I grew together. It became a
part of me, an extension of my thoughts and desires,
the muscular reactions which put them into effect, and,
indeed, of my very personality. In the same way,
when I was driving her, I seemed to become part of
the car. I was finely bred. I had good manners. I was
enormously strong, but completely restrained. Oddly
enough, other people noticed this. I became associated
with the car, as if we had a joint personality. Only the
other day, I met a Cambridge professor who had been
ten years in Australia, and the first thing he said to me
was, 'Are you still running that Rolls?'

Daily, for five days a week, I expended seven gallons
of petrol in travelling to and from London. Once we
were chased through the streets of London by not less
than five police cars at the same time. Looking back on
it, I find the memory rather amusing. But the odd thing
is that I believe I even found it amusing at the time.
What happened was this.

It was at the time when Burgess and Maclean had
set the whole world by the ears by suddenly disappearing from the Foreign Office, where they worked,
and turning up in Moscow, where they were later
joined by Philby. We were approached one day by an
148   extraordinarily little Italian American, who, if one

could judge from the bulges in each armpit, and in various other parts of an extremely tight-fitting suit, was armed to the teeth. He had a hair-line moustache. He walked in unannounced, and said that he was a member of what he called 'The Organization', and had a special message for us from Guy Burgess. He told us that the organization was in touch with Burgess, who was convinced now that he had made a frightful mistake, and wanted to be got out of Russia, so that he could spend the rest of his life in Switzerland. Since he knew my joint Managing Director slightly, and we were the only publishers he could think of, the message was that if we could help him to escape, he offered us the book in payment. The little man pulled up his trousers to preserve the creases and sat down delicately in our one comfortable chair, and waited for us to say something.

We didn't say a thing. We darted glances at each other, and began trembling.

Now you must understand that the excitement about the Burgess and Maclean thing had reached such a pitch, that if this was true, it seemed that we were being handed the scoop of the century.

'O.K., so you don't believe me.'

'Do you mean that your organization, as you call it, can go in and out of Russia at will?'

'Nope. The Organization don't cross any frontiers. It passes small pieces of paper through the barriers, and the next man takes it from there. Do you want that we should give a demonstration?'

'That would be helpful, Mister—'

'You can call me Faranetti.'

'It would be helpful, Mr Faranetti.'

'Send him a message. Send him a trick message. Send him something nobody else in the world will 149 understand, let alone any Russians. Write it on a small piece of paper, screw it up tight, and you'll have an answer in ten days. Howzat?' He rose to his full five feet, four inches, went to the door, and turned. Suddenly the hair-line moustache split in a reptilian grin.

'Don't look so scared, fellas. Same time tomorrow?'

We weren't scared. The pallor was pure nervous excitement. We knew a man in Ladbroke Grove who had been collaborating with Guy Burgess on a book, in the middle of which he had disappeared. The book was a biography of Lady Gwendolyn Cecil, the daughter of the Victorian Lord Salisbury. There must be something in that book, some order of words, some little recollection of work done together, that only the two collaborators would recognize.

Without another word, we put on our hats and coats, went downstairs, got into the Rolls, and drove off to Ladbroke Grove.

I don't know if you know Ladbroke Grove? It's an extremely respectable neighbourhood, with a great many trees, and it rises at quite a sharp angle from Holland Park Avenue, deteriorating as it goes, until it becomes one of the worst slums in London.

We told our story, and our man became as excited as we were. He sat down at a Corona typewriter with a blue ribbon, and tapped out the following message.

'Are you still interested in Lady Gwendolyn?'

We thought that was absolutely perfect. We folded it up until it was about the size of an Oxo cube, and on the following day we placed it in the claw-like hand of Mr Faranetti.

Ten days later, Mr Faranetti arrived and produced, after some searching, from his handkerchief pocket another piece of paper, similarly typed in blue ribbon

on a portable machine.

'Yes, I am still interested in "The Plain".'

This didn't mean a thing to us, but our distinguished writer in Ladbroke Grove trembled like a jelly when he read it.

'Old Victorian joke,' he explained. 'Lady G was an ugly girl, so they called her "Salisbury Plain". Only Guy could possibly have known that.'

Well that put us in a tizzy, as you may expect. We rushed round to a newspaper called *The People* and sold them the serial rights for a £100,000.

This would put Burgess, one gathers, in the Harold Wilson class. In those days it was, undoubtedly, a record price. I drove back to Peaslake. And then something rather alarming happened. I found that my telephone was being tapped. The Police didn't have tape recorders in those days, and I could clearly hear the elaborate noises of a large constable doing his best to hold his breath. I then found that if I telephoned the garage, their telephone was tapped too. And when I telephoned my father in Shamley Green, the stertorous breathing was loud and clear. I began to feel genuinely frightened. I was no traitor to my country, and the last thing I wanted was to find myself bracketed with two men who were. So I rang Ladbroke Grove.

'I believe the Police are on to this thing.'

'Oh?'

'They're tapping my phone. And after this I've no doubt they'll start tapping yours.'

There was a long pause.

Presently, in a very different voice, he asked, 'What do you propose to do?'

'Call the whole ruddy thing off, I think. Can I come and talk to you?'

'Of course.'

'I'll be with you in an hour.'

I clambered nervously into the Rolls, slid the seat on to its proper catch, and we went off together at considerable speed.

It really takes an hour and twenty minutes to get to London from Peaslake. But at exactly one hour after starting we drew up outside the flat. Two large black Wolseleys were standing there, both facing up the hill but one on either side of the road. They had illuminated signs saying 'POLICE' on the roof. We were expected!

Our man seemed curiously pleased and excited by all this. He took me to the window.

'How many Police cars can you see?'

'Two.'

'Actually there are five.'

'I make it two.'

'Look at the aerials.'

He was absolutely right.

Outside, a small laundry van, with 'Somebody or Other's Laundry' painted on the sides, had an immense Police aerial sticking out of its roof. A small sports M.G. had the same, arising from its back bumper. Further up the road a very pedestrian-looking Morris was similarly equipped.

'There's a man in the telephone box too.'

'My God, so there is!'

'I think this is frightfully funny.'

'I'm fed up to the teeth.'

'Have some tea. It's Lapsang Souchong.'

'You realize that they heard me say on the telephone that I was coming?'

'Heavy breathing. No sugar, I take it?'

'No thanks. Well I'm going to ring up Scotland Yard and call the whole thing off.'

'Yes. I suppose you've got to. It seems a pity. Are they going to chase you?'

152

'Looks like it.'

'Why don't you lead a funeral procession?'

'That's a frightfully good idea! In fact I'll do it now. Watch!'

I drank the rest of my tea and went downstairs and got in to the car. Five starters whirred in unison. But only five. I paused to light a cigarette very slowly and carefully. Then I started the engine and moved the car about a foot. In a split second of time, the two Police Wolseleys with a howl of acceleration and a scream of tyres started up the hill at what I can only describe as 80 mph.

I went a further ten yards, stopped and reversed into a mews. The Wolseleys could be seen about a quarter of a mile away, with heads sticking out of windows. They too began to back around.

I put my right flipper up, and proceeded in modest fashion to the confluence with Holland Park Avenue. By now the two Wolseleys were in line behind. The man was leaving the telephone box and getting into the laundry van, after which they all took up station in line astern.

A thoroughly evil idea came in to my head. I felt pretty confident that, with all their bustle and confusion, I could beat the two Wolseleys easily in straight acceleration from a standstill. What I wanted, in fact, was a traffic situation in which there was room for one car to cross the road, but not more than one. I thought the Police would probably sound their gongs, but if I chose precisely the right moment when the two streams of traffic travelling in opposite directions made a simultaneous gap, through which I could dive headlong, the moving traffic would almost certainly plug the gap before they had time to stop.

This was going to be a very difficult and delicate operation. Very delicate indeed. It was going to be like

153

fencing. The quick lunge to the heart before anybody
could see what was happening. As it happened, I
could see that my chance was not more than fifty
yards away. To my right, a heavy lorry was lumbering
up the incline, with a gap in front of it. To the left,
two enormous carthorses slipped and slithered down
the hill with a load of beer behind them and a string
of infuriated motorists trying unsuccessfully to pass.
And nobody in front. If those two gaps arrived simultaneously, now was my chance! Now was the moment!
The gap opened in front of me. I banged my foot
down and we shot forward. There was one hell of a
noise of gongs and sirens, and when I looked in the
mirror, all five Police cars were still on the other side
of the road. The only thing to do, it seemed, was to
wait for them. So I carefully drew in to the kerb and
waited, leaving insufficient room for more than one or
two cars behind me. The chase was on.

They stopped the traffic all right. The two Wolseleys
crossed and came to a halt behind me. The laundry
van, the M.G. and the Morris turned right into the
traffic and were lost to view.

I sat there smoking my cigarette for, perhaps, half a
minute. I then extended my left flipper, put the car in
motion, and, at about 10 mph, not more, took the first
turning to the left. Still at 10 mph, I extended my
right flipper and took the next turning to the right. I
was very near where I used to buy that methanol, so
I knew those streets. At the next intersection, ahead, I
suddenly saw the three Q-cars buzzing busily across
like mosquitoes.

We travelled down Abbotsbury Road, turned left
into Melbury Road, always at 10 mph and always with
the appropriate flipper in action.

154   Twenty yards later the foremost Police car

Above: *1934 Rolls-Royce Phantom II*
M.M.M.

Below: *1936 8-cylinder Mercedes-Benz 540K*
M.M.M.

*Hitler smiles at
Hermann and
Emmy Göring in
their Mercedes-Benz
just after their
wedding in Berlin
Cathedral, 10 April
1935*
LONDON EXPRESS

Above: *1936 3½-litre Derby*
Bentley with semi-convertible body by
Gurney Nutting
M.M.M.

Below: *1936*
Hispano–Suiza K6
sports saloon
M.M.M.

Right: *1937 Cord 812 supercharged phaeton*
M.M.M.

Below: *The author's 1933 6-cylinder 7-litre Rolls-Royce Continental Phantom II with body by Freestone and Webb*

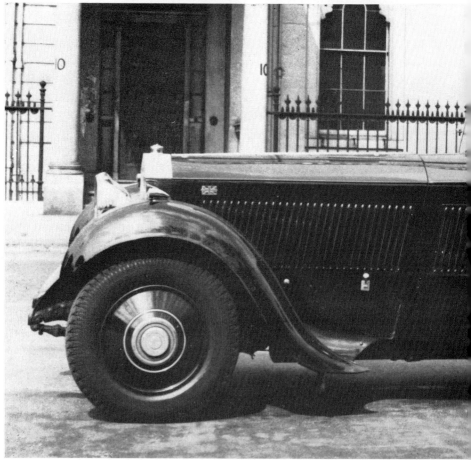

Left: *1937 4-cylinder 1½-litre Singer entered for the Welsh Rally* M.M.M.

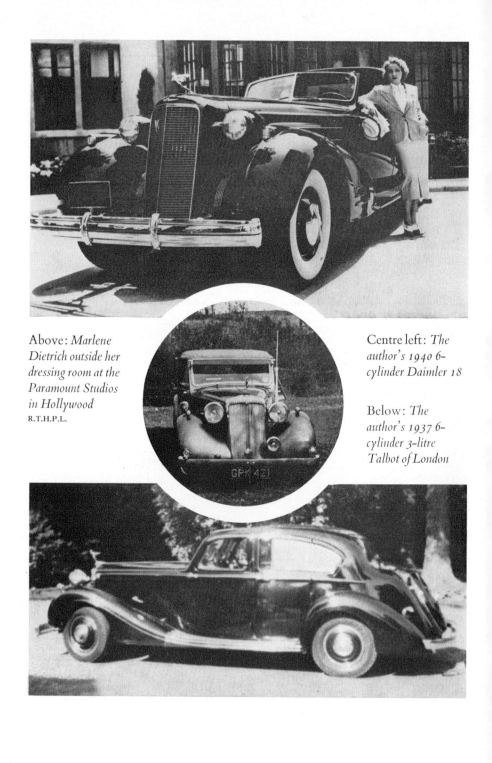

Above: *Marlene
Dietrich outside her
dressing room at the
Paramount Studios
in Hollywood*
R.T.H.P.L.

Centre left: *The
author's 1940 6-
cylinder Daimler 18*

Below: *The
author's 1937 6-
cylinder 3-litre
Talbot of London*

left: *1962 Goggomobile T3 saloon*
M.M.M.

Below: *Nubar Gulbenkian's coachbuilt taxi*
LONDON EXPRESS

The author's 1962
8-cylinder 2700 cc
Daimler SP250

accelerated past me and drew in to the kerb, so bringing me to a halt. A policeman got out, walked back
and stuck his head through the window.

'What's the matter with you?' he demanded.

'The matter?' I echoed, tapping a little cigarette ash
on to the roadway.

'Yes. What's the matter?'

'Nothing.'

'But—but—'

'I'm in no hurry, that's all.'

'Our instructions are to see where you're going.'

'You really needn't bother to come, I can tell you
that—12 Beauchamp Place.'

'What's that?'

'My office.'

'12 Beauchamp Place?'

'That's right. You've already got one man in the
office, another man examining the corsets in the street,
and a third in the pub opposite. They can soon tell you
when I arrive. We don't really have to do everything at
80 mph, you know.'

I never saw a man more disgusted and disappointed.
His face was pale with frustration. He got back in to
his car and drove away. The car behind me drove
away too. I suppose they used their aerials.

Still strictly adhering to my funereal pace, and using
my flipper obsequiously, I turned down into Kensington High Street, went down Queen's Gate, and made
my way to Lennox Gardens. Then I walked back to the
office, and telephoned Scotland Yard.

That evening as I arrived at Peaslake, the telephone
bell was ringing. It was the lady from the exchange.

'It's all right,' she said. 'He's gorn.'

We went all over the place together, the Rolls and I,   155

fleet-footed and always sure. We climbed the moun-
tains. That includes Geneva. And that was one of the
few places where our personalities diverged. For I
cannot stand heights. I am not really happy at more
than a hundred feet above sea-level. The house I
live in is 400 feet high, and it makes me pant, and
become bad tempered and a rotten sleeper. Whereas
on the Devonshire coast, to which we repair every
summer, I can run up and down hills and am geniality
itself and nothing on earth will keep me awake, night
or day. This fantastic mountain very nearly did for me.
I felt as though I was going to explode in all directions,
that my eyes were going to pop out of my head, that all
my liquids would suddenly emerge at various orifices;
whereas the old Rolls made the ascent commandingly,
with never a whimper.

It was at a Swiss customs point down below, when I
was gradually pulling myself together again, that the
officer demanded something he called my 'green
card'.

I had never heard of a green card. In the good old
days, one travelled under the auspices of the R.A.C.
with a bundle of documents in a neat cardboard
folder, and I had never even looked at them to see
what they were. The customs man spoke the most
perfect English.

'When an English gentleman travels abroad in his
carriage,' he said, 'he is supposed to carry a green card.
I will make you one myself.'

When we parked the car outside the Hotel Beau
Rivage, in Geneva, for a cup of tea and piece of currant
cake, an instant crowd collected. And when I stopped
at a garage round the corner to get some petrol and oil,
and opened the bonnet to display that vast engine,
which looked capable of propelling a Channel steamer

at twenty knots, they were aghast with astonishment,
and one splendid man exclaimed, '*Ah! Quel morceau*
de puissance!'

It's no good pretending that since the car and I were
one I didn't enjoy this sort of thing.

We had my father on board, as well as my daughter,
and the object of the expedition was to see somebody
at the University of Grenoble and arrange for her to
do a few terms there. And, with that business arranged,
to drop down to the Mediterranean coast. We even
saw a beckoning signpost reading 'Nice 57 kilometres'.
But we had reckoned without my father.

My father hated motorcars. 'Why can't people take
a nice, comfortable train?' They made him cantankerous. By Grenoble he was so cantankerous that
he absolutely refused to continue. We had to yield, of
course. I am sure it was further on the map, but that is
what we were doing in Geneva. We drove the few
extra miles into Annecy, and there we found a very
nice little hotel on the borders of the lake, which
proudly called itself the Hôtel Robinson. We booked
in, as we thought, for a single night, hoping that when
my father had had a good night's sleep, we could
prevail upon him to travel the last two hours to the
Mediterranean.

Not a bit of it.

In the morning, he pointed out that every mile
travelled further south was another mile to be
travelled on the way home. As if each mile was a nail
in his coffin. He declared firmly that he was going to
stay in the Robinson until it was time to make for home.

So stay we did.

Annecy is a nice little place. I like bathing in lakes
better than bathing in the sea. I like to explore
unbroken waters. I like to disturb the peace myself, 157

instead of letting other people disturb it for me. But after one's bathe and the stoking up on the local fish, there was absolutely nothing else in Annecy to do. I believe there was a cinema, but we never went to it. We grew to know the outsides, and many of the insides, of the local shops. There was a sort of no-man's land between Switzerland and France where you could buy dutiable goods free of duty. This didn't do anybody any good because we had to declare them later. There is always a temptation to smuggle, and of course it is easier with a Rolls-Royce than carrying one's luggage through a customs shed, and slapping it on the table in front of a man. There are so many places to put things.

After three or four days, the weather changed. It changed with extraordinary suddenness and violence. One morning there was snow on all the surrounding hills and the water in the lake turned near to ice. The small changing hut, maintained by the hotel at the water's edge, was folded up and taken away. We were very sad about this because, even though it would have been impossible to enter the water, the sun was still strong enough for a sun bathe. We made representations to the principal Robinson. But he was adamant. On 15 September the cabin must be removed.

'C'est le fin de saison, Monsieur.'

Then the hotel itself began to grow colder. As a purely summer resort, it was not furnished with any sort of heating whatever. At the end of the month it would close its shutters, lock all its doors, draw its blinds and all the Robinsons depart for Paris.

It got colder and colder. It got so cold that I used to fill my wash basin with the hottest possible water, and hope that the small amount of steam would help to raise the temperature of the room a little.

My father suffered the worst. He was very susceptible to pneumonia, and we were extremely worried. We had only to enter the car, drive for no time at all and find blazing temperatures, with everybody in bikinis. He preferred to sit, huddled in his room, wearing an overcoat, shivering and smoking innumerable cigarettes, and refusing to budge until Friday.

We had a word with the management. My wife does this sort of thing very well. She mentioned that my father was a very distinguished man, with a title, and that he was also a Chevalier de la Légion d'Honneur. So the management did finally produce a distinctly tatty electric fire, with loose wires dangling all over it. It worked, and all we had to do was to sit the holiday out.

Now, to equip us properly for the journey, I had acquired from Messrs Paddon four impressive-looking Dunlop re-treads. Almost invariably something goes wrong on these occasions, and the wise man takes steps to prevent adding tyre trouble to the other possibilities.

On Friday we set forth for home, with the luggage loaded into the boot, the tyres pumped up hard to carry it and thirty-seven gallons in the tank. Our aim was to go to Paris, whistle up a few friends, accept an invitation to a damned good dinner from them, spend the night, and cross from Dieppe to Newhaven the following day.

The first half of the journey was completely uneventful. My daughter was driving. I was relaxing in the back, and basking in the warmth of the heater I had fitted there, on the theory that it is the people at the back who suffer most from the cold, and not the driver, who has a hot engine in front of his legs. My daughter always drives too fast. It is perfectly all right

to keep up a steady 65 mph along the straight French
roads, but not, I fancy, through towns and villages.
The French do it, of course, but the French have some
very peculiar cars. They have absolutely no power
whatever, but are at the same time quite remarkably
fast. I don't know how the French manage this, but
the effect on travel is somewhat disturbing! On a mild
upward slope, the Rolls would flash nonchalantly past
thirty or forty of these ridiculous minnows. After
breasting the slight hill and going into a gentle
declivity on the other side, the whole brood would
come roaring and puffing triumphantly past, doing a
xenophobic seventy to a man.

After passing one of those giant *camions* on the way,
we became aware of the fact that the amount of noise
the driver was making was specially directed at us. He
was sounding off on two separate horns, shouting at the
top of his voice, and pointing at the car. The back-seat
passengers could see his distorted face.

'Better stop,' my wife said. 'Stop, Frances! Stop,
Frances!'

She pulled in decorously to the right side of the
road, with a click of the handbrake. The lorry driver
thundered past, waving, shouting and pointing, all at
once.

'*Vous êtes en panne, Mademoiselle,*' he bawled.

'Isn't that the French for break-down?'

'Better let me have a look,' I said.

Come to think of it, I had noticed a curious slapping
sound. I got out and walked round the car. And there,
on the outside rear wheel, was an enormous balloon-
like bulge, the size of an Israeli melon. Those brand-
new Dunlop re-treads! We all got out and stood
disconsolately around the car. The wolf pack chortled
past.

'I cannot understand,' my father said, 'why people can't travel in a nice, comfortable train.'

There was obviously nothing for it but to get down on one's haunches and change the wheel. Fortunately, in those dim distant days, the jack lived under the bonnet, and the spare wheel was sticking out at the back. At least we were spared the post-war necessity of scattering our luggage all over the roadside. The only real difficulty was the enormous weight of the wheel. They were wire wheels with Ace discs over them, and to get them off, you had to attach a tremendous Whitworth spanner, and clout it with a copper hammer. You unscrewed a very fine thread by about twenty-five turns. You then tried to pull the wheel towards you along a great many splines. Usually it resisted at first, and then came suddenly, so that you fell over backwards with the wheel on top of you. This reminds me of a story of the Bishop of Guildford.

The Bishop of Guildford used to take delight in touring the Surrey countryside on foot, dressed in his full episcopal robes with a mitre on his head and a crozier in his hand. On one of his walks he came across a lorry driver, who was doing exactly what I was doing, trying to tug a wheel off its bearings and using all the four-letter words in the English language.

'My man,' said the Bishop. 'You really mustn't say things like that.'

The man stood up, puffing, sweating and panting.

'Well, what do I say?'

'Say "Please God, help me to get this wheel off."'

'O.K.,' the man said. 'I'll give it a try.'

He got down on his haunches again and said, 'Please God, help me to get this wheel off.' It came off in his hands.

'Well,' the Bishop said, 'I'll be God-damned!'

While I was still struggling, one of those small Citroëns drove past and came to a halt about fifty yards away. A father and his three sons got out.

'I believe they're going to help us,' my wife said.

'I don't need any help.'

She began to walk towards them with her most engaging smile. All four stood together in serried rank, and relieved themselves by the side of the road. Then they buttoned up, climbed into the car again, and drove away without giving us a single glance.

I must not belabour you with overmuch description. I got the wheel changed, and with the whole of the front of my suit in a most awful mess, I took the driver's seat, thinking we would proceed with cat-like tread, at a very gentle pace indeed, to give those tyres a chance to cool down. So off we went, with a phut, phut, phut. From the back of the car.

It took me almost a mile, before the horrid thought struck me that the phut, phut, phutting should have been cured. I pulled up as gently as possible and got down to see. Sure enough, the other rear wheel had a balloon on it, this time, the size of a small orange, but heart-sinking nevertheless. It began to be apparent that we were not going to be able to drive the two hundred miles into Paris.

'I cannot understand,' my father said, 'why you people cannot travel in a nice, comfortable train.'

The nice, comfortable train syndrome seemed, at that moment, the only possible means of escape from this wilderness in the middle of France. But where was it? The train, I mean. And there was another little matter which raised its head. We had our tickets back for the car and its passengers from Dieppe to Newhaven, and just enough money to cover us, with a bit over for that one night in Paris. We hadn't anything like enough

money to buy first-class tickets on a Paris train, and
then more tickets from Paris to Dieppe, and then,
possibly, fresh tickets on the boat. The idea of buying
four new tyres was out of the question. The only course
open to us was to go limping along at 20 mph, and
hope that the car would somehow or other get us to
Paris, even if it took us all night.

By the most astonishing coincidence, I just recently
found in one of my untidy drawers a scrumpled piece
of paper, which I had not seen from that day to this.

'Garage Modern,' it said.

'M. W. Jed Rejewski.'

'Cravant.'

'Yonne.'

That was where the right-hand tyre quietly lowered
itself to ground level in the very forecourt of M.
Rejewski's garage, which, in its turn, was in a little
semicircle of shops, grouped around a country railway
station.

I think it was this invitation to the railway network of
France which induced us to make a whole chain of
serious blunders. But there was the railway station.
There was the little café next door, which supplied us
at a moment's notice with four remarkably good
omelettes, and lashings of coffee. And there was my
father, wistfully watching the signals and listening to
the snort of trains.

So, after the omelettes, we asked M. Rejewski to
look after the car, and staggered with our very heavy
luggage into the station and over an enormously high
bridge, to the platform on the other side.

It is an extraordinary thing, but my futile brain was
busying itself with wondering how long I could tote a
steamer trunk and remain alive, and how I could
purchase some new tyres and whether or not I could   163

then take them down by train, on the following morning to Cravant, rescue the car, dash back to Paris, in
time to get the R.A.C. there to defer the boat passage
till the following day. This crazy scheme was, actually,
what I decided to do. At that moment in time, as
everybody now says, we were thoroughly preoccupied
with physical endurance.

In order to get to Paris, we had to take a little single-
carriage motorized affair to a more important station.
We stood on the platform waiting for it, still trembling
from our exertions over the luggage. When it bustled
in, making impatient noises on its hooter, it was
completely full, and we were forced to lift up all our
luggage again and push it in among a lot of people
standing near the door, who didn't appear too pleased
to receive it. Then we clambered in ourselves, too
white-faced to care about the hostile mutterings. In
the next second we dieseled off, leaving my poor car,
my alter ego, where it stood.

I have forgotten the name of the town we came to,
but my father insisted that third-class tickets should
be bought. I agreed to this, on condition that we used
them to stand in the corridor of the first-class com-
partments. This we did, humping that infernal
luggage once again, and found we were on that famous
train that travels to Paris from Switzerland at a steady
speed of 85 mph. The track was continuous. The steel
wheels gave a high-pitched unvarying scream. We
did the 200 miles in two hours and twenty minutes.

I thought there was something to be said for the
nice comfortable train.

Paris is civilized. There are porters and taxis. The
unpleasant feeling of being a helpless refugee, stranded
with one's luggage, was brushed away, like cobwebs.
164 We went to a hotel in the Place Vendôme. It was loud

with American voices. My father rang up the Paris
Editor of the *New York Times*, and borrowed £100
from him. We also got that invitation to dinner. It was
still only teatime. There is another address written on
the back of that crumpled piece of paper.

'R.A.C.'

'8, Place Vendôme.'

I walked over. The man was a Frenchman but he
spoke remarkably good English.

'Monsieur?'

'Oh, good afternoon. Whereabouts in Paris can I buy
some tyres for a Rolls-Royce Phantom II Continental?'

'Nowhere, Monsieur.'

'But surely—'

'You probably have the only Rolls-Royce Phantom
II Continental in the whole of France.'

'What about that place in the Champs Elysées?'

'They will be prepared to sell you a motorcar for
F200,000, Monsieur. But not tyres for a Phantom II.
What year is it?'

'1933.'

He spread his hands, palms upward and went
through the motions of weighing an explanation
which he found wanting.

'H'm,' I said miserably.

'You could have some flown out, Monsieur. It
would be not inexpensive, but you should be able to
get them in two or three days.'

'Well, that's part of the trouble. You see we've got
tickets for the Newhaven boat tomorrow, and we've
run out of money, and if we can't use them—'

He interrupted me.

'Where is the car, Monsieur?'

I told him, 'Garage Modern. M. W. Jed Rejewski.
Cravant, Yonne.'

He wrote it all carefully down on a piece of paper:
I strongly suspect *this* piece of paper. It must have
come back with the documents.

'Would you allow me to advise you, sir? Travel with
your passengers on the Newhaven boat tomorrow,
already paid for, and leave us to rescue the car. It is
one of the free services of the R.A.C.'

I made the face of an idiot.

'We are doing it all the time. The moment you
came in at the door . . .' He left the rest of the sentence
as a series of dots.

'I hate to leave the car. But, very well. I suppose so.'

He smiled. 'Thank you, Mr Gibbs.'

Three or four days later, I was driven down to
Newhaven in the Singer. There was my Rolls, standing
on the dockside, dirty, forlorn, and looking rebellious,
I thought, as if she didn't want to look me in the eye.
If she had been a horse, I suppose I would have
patted her neck, like those female steeplechasers. I did
tap a finger on her bonnet. It made no difference.
Then I noticed she was standing on four tyres. And
beside her was a man dressed in mufti, but with some
indication that he belonged to the R.A.C. He was
wearing either a cap or an armband. I forget which.

'Did you fetch her?'

'Yessir.'

'However did you manage about tyres?'

'Had them repaired, sir. Are you the owner of this
vehicle? Would you sign here, please.'

I signed there and poured pound notes into his
hand. At least two.

So we drove home again, the Rolls and I. A strange
barrier had grown up between us. I was not going to
be forgiven. In the first place, everything that could be
stolen from the car had been stolen. The cubbyholes

were empty. The tartan rug had gone. So had a very ingenious and rather expensive route-map that could be altered by jabbing extensions at the side, so that the road unfolded as one travelled along it. Then the petrol gauge failed. This was the only time in a tenure of three Rolls-Royces and two Bentleys that I have ever known anything actually fail to function. Then the pipe to the rear water heater, which was fixed to the chassis by a coil of wire, came adrift. The wire curled itself round the propeller shaft and the fiendish tappings and slitherings sounded like a horde of ghosts. It was the very next day, after I had put in a routine appearance in London, and was driving myself home down the King's Road, that a car pulled up beside me at the very same traffic lights and an American voice shouted across at me, 'Say, will you sell me that car?'

This must have been foreordained.

'Yes,' I said.

When the lights changed, I pulled into that garage on the right. He drew in behind me. He had one of those derisory early post-war American cars. A coach-builder's nightmare, with emblematic rockets down the sides and sixteen tail lamps.

We walked into the showrooms together.

'This gentleman wants to buy my car. How much do you think I ought to charge him for it?'

'Phantom II?'

'Continental.'

'Year?'

'Thirty-three.'

'Oh . . . £300.'

'O.K.,' I said.

The man started peeling off travellers' cheques.

The next day, I met a man called Scott-Moncrieff at a cocktail party. I told him what had happened, not

knowing that he was one of the greatest experts on
pre-war Rolls-Royces.

'I could have got you £3,000,' he said quietly.

Today, it could be worth—what, £7,000? But I
would rather be driving it. I still carry its picture in
my pocket. It was, after all, queen of the greatest
period in motoring.

CHAPTER IX

The Last Daimler

WITH £300 JINGLING in one's pocket what sort of car could one buy in this beautiful post-war world?

Let us survey the scene.

If you had approximately £7,000 to spend you could, indeed, still buy a Rolls-Royce or a Bentley. But they were not quite the same thing as before, were they? The Bentley emerged from the war as the Standard Steel Saloon. Even the Rolls-Royce, now known if I remember as The Dawn, appeared in the same utilitarian guise. For one reason or another, the coach-builder, who brought a touch of artistry to his craft, had been blasted from the scene. The only names 169

which remained were those specialist firms which had
been bought up and kept alive by the manufacturer.
The root cause of this catastrophe was that some un-
caring nonentity had discovered that the chassis was
no longer necessary. You could build a perfectly
workmanlike car by buying a few sheets of thin steel,
shoving them under a monolithic press, stamping
them into the rough outline of a motorcar, and, with a
bit of strengthening here and there, stick an engine in
front, a wheel at each corner, and drive them off the
assembly line at the rate of one every eight seconds.

Confronted with these tin canisters, the coach-
builder could do nothing. If they cut off only the roof,
the whole thing fell to pieces in their hands. It was
impossible to build a decent body because there was
nothing on which to build. In the fifties and sixties,
what was there?

Well, if you couldn't afford the Rolls-Royce Dawn
or the Bentley Standard Steel Saloon, but still had
quite a lot of money, you could buy a Lagonda. It was
not, of course, W. O. Bentley's V-Twelve Lagonda,
and it had the Bristol engine. Prince Philip bought one
and they had a reputation, no doubt undeserved, for
unreliability. There were Daimlers still being made
with Wilson gearboxes—that model was known as
The Consort—but they were all the same, and very
dowdy they looked. The Alvis was rather a well-
made car. So was the Rover. But both carried the
badge of 'pre-war', until the Rover suddenly appeared
with one headlight in the middle of its radiator,
looking exactly like the last electric tram.

There was, of course, the Jaguar. But I didn't like,
and never have liked, the Jaguar line. It bears too close
a resemblance to the banana. Whatever happened to
Sir William Lyons of Austin Swallow fame? They

tended to be driven by rather unpleasant people, because they had a performance quite out of keeping with
the cost and with the times. In nine cases out of ten,
if you came across a pile-up on the road there was a
Jaguar at the bottom of it.

I am afraid we have to pass judgement that not one
of these machines could hold a candle to the really
great cars of the pre-war era. There wasn't a gentleman's carriage among the lot of them. If it comes to
that, there were no longer any gentlemen. The roads
became filled with Standard Vanguards and the
products of the giant manufacturers, the growing
empires of Lord Nuffield and the American empires of
Ford and Vauxhall. It was a social revolution. These
cars poured out from the factories, literally in millions,
designed to be bought by the millions on hire-
purchase. Like everything else in life, the fashion in
motorcars, instead of spreading downwards from the
top, began to come up from below. Long hair and the
sidewhisker, the appalling cacophony of pop music,
the tattered jeans, the shirt worn outside the trousers,
the pronunciation, the faults in grammar like 'He
invited my wife and I to a party', the mini-skirt, the
pornography, the contempt for marriage, the un-
washed look, the hatless brigade, holidays on the
Costa Brava—none of these things have spread down
from 'the nobs', but many have been adopted by
them.

So it was—and is—with the motorcar. The mouth-
organ front, with the lamp each end or, in very special
cases, two lamps, is now worn with a certain amount of
over-ornamentation by the Rover and the Aston
Martin.

The trouble is that all these cars look identical, like
the Japanese. If a million or so of one make comes out

with a spavined body, then by the next motor show all cars have spavined bodies. The only thing that the private owner can do who wants to add a touch of originality, is to flaunt some accessories. At the time I sold my Rolls, every car in the kingdom had something called a 'bug deflector' on the bonnet. This was a pair of transparent plastic wings designed to keep the windscreen out of the main air stream. I haven't seen any for years. But I have seen plenty of cars with imitation magnesium wheels with the letters GT or TC and double exhaust pipes and yellow number plates. Why does anybody want their number plate to be visible in the dark? I should have thought it more appropriate to invent one that was invisible in the day-time.

To everyone who remembers the shapeliness of the Golden Age, the drabness of present-day design is depressing to the point of salt tears. The Big Three, who have to all intents and purposes bought up every marque on the market, appear not to bother. That man Issigonis, who designed the Mini, talks of 'two boxes' and 'three boxes'. What a deplorable approach to beauty! Yet in five minutes I could transform the Mini into quite a pretty little car at a cost of not more than two shillings an item—if you will forgive my mentioning something so obsolescent as two shillings. It is basically a question of removing those totally unnecessary sloping exterior welds, removing that gutter behind at the back and taking it down behind the rear windows, so that it looks a little less like Beatrice d'Este, and lowering the back to the level of the sides so that it doesn't seem to travel with its tail up. In this sad procession of vehicles designed by people in Coventry and Birmingham and similar centres of good taste, only the 'Farina-bodied Austins and Morrises linger with an air of good proportions.

Which brings me to the car I did buy. It was a one-off exercise by Pininfarina on a six-cylinder Fiat chassis. It was a most remarkable object. Its main feature was that its prow, sticking out three feet ahead of the front wheels, including the radiator, the lamp glasses and the wings, formed a complete hemisphere. To achieve this effect, the lamp glasses, in order to follow the same curvature, had to be two feet wide. The result was amazing. A man in Guildford, when I stopped beside him, cried 'Oh no!' But if a man from Mars, who had never in his life seen a motorcar of any other shape, was suddenly presented with this example of man's ingenuity and charm, he would probably have clapped his claws together. This vast overhang and overall width, coupled with the fact that the wind-screen was in its classic position of halfway between the axles, meant that when you raised the bonnet you were confronted with an acreage that made the Mathis appear crammed with machinery.

'You could hold a dance in there,' said the first man who filled me up with oil. The whole thing was painted a rather unpleasant khaki colour with an orange roof made of plastic, so that there was no possibility whatever of anybody mistaking it for a Morris Minor, or a Ford Popular, or even an Alvis Silver Lady. The roof opened, but it was a mistake to put this to the test, because every time you did so the orange paint which some extrovert had applied stuck together in the folds, and showed a tendency to adhere to the adjacent piece when you endeavoured to effect a closure. I bought it from a man on the *Express*. I think I paid him £200.

He promised to deliver it to me at Beauchamp Place on Friday, and when Friday came and passed without the car I got him on the telephone, and he told me it

had broken its back axle in the middle of Fleet Street.
I didn't pay much attention to this at the time. After
all, a broken back axle could happen to anybody. It
was then, on the following Tuesday when I accepted
delivery and handed over the shekels, that I began to
appreciate the fascinating habits of this vehicle. It
broke its back axle in the fast lane of the Kingston
By-pass when I was taking it home.

That was a very strange experience, which I had
never before undergone. It happened when I was
braking with some violence at a light which had turned
against me. I inserted my second gear, ready for the
take-off, and when the lights changed a great deal of
mechanism could be heard revolving very sweetly,
whereas no actual movement of the car took place. It
was oddly pleasant. I could have sat there indefinitely,
listening to that vibrationless engine. But the other
traffic did not approve. Fortunately there was a
policeman stationed near the lights, ready to pounce
upon possible offenders.

'Something the matter, sir?' he enquired, with the
merest trace of sarcasm.

'I don't seem to make any progress.'

'Have you got a gear engaged, sir, if I *may* ask?'

'Yes, of course! Look!'

'I'm very much afraid that means a broken back axle.'

'But the axle was only mended this morning.'

'Probably the other half, sir. It often happens in
pairs.'

'You astonish me. Will you help give me a shove?'

We pushed it into a service road, where there was a
bright red telephone box and I was able to ring for
rescue.

Not for the last time.

I managed to get through to a Fiat expert just north

of the Park who had been recommended by the chap on the *Express* as holding spares for every possible variation of Fiat. When I arrived on the end of a piece of rope and he saw the car, he laughed with a strange excitement. He opened the bonnet.

'I thought so! Just like the one I had before the war. There's that ghastly thermostat. You'll have trouble with that, once every few weeks. And the core plugs are always coming out. Have the springs broken yet? They will. And as for the armatures on the dynamo and starter motor . . .'

'Did you say, "before the war"?'

'Oh Lord, yes. They used the chassis for a time during the war, as a little military runabout. Sort of Italian jeep. Look, there's their mark where the wireless transmitter was fitted. Probably travelled miles over the desert sand.'

'But why would Pininfarina use his special one-off experimental body on a jeep?'

'Cheap, I suppose. Anyhow, leave it with me.'

I left it with him. And when, three or four days later, I collected it, in working order, I discovered to my astonishment that the other voyagers of the road were convinced that I was in something really fast. Two Jaguars pulled over to the left and waved me on. Fortunately this happened where the hill slopes gently down into Leatherhead. If we had been going the other way I should never have made it. It was getting dark, and when I turned off the main road at Effingham to cross the Downs, which was my own private way to Peaslake, I had to turn on the headlights. Just as I was passing the convent which the good nuns had turned into quite a fashionable girls' school, the lights went out. I stopped with a bang. So, without the bang, did the engine. When I turned the key, the starter was mute. There was, in fact, no electricity of any sort left anywhere in the car.

I went in to the small lodge at the convent gates and explained my predicament to a very charming woman, who invited me to use her telephone and offered me cups of tea. After about half an hour's awkward conversation, the car from the Peaslake garage arrived, with a long length of rope. After much snorting and grunting we got all the knots tied and set forth in procession. We had scarcely travelled more than half a mile, when I decided that I could hold the rope taut all right if we went a trifle faster. And in order to attract the attention of the car ahead, I gave him a blast on the horn.

His name was Hutchings and he was the owner of the garage, but everyone called him Jack—Jack stopped the car and came over.

'That's funny.'

'What's funny?'

'That horn sounded!'

'Good Lord! So it did.'

'Try everything else.'

I tried everything else. Horn, lights, starter, cigar-lighter, interior light, windscreen wipers, all worked perfectly.

'Are you sure you had everything turned on? There's a master switch.'

'Master switch?'

'Down there.'

'I didn't even know I had one.'

'That's funny.'

'What's funny?'

'It's turned off.'

'Whichever way it works, I assure you I didn't touch it, I didn't even know it was there.'

'Well, try turning it off.'

I flipped the switch.

The engine continued to run. The lights remained alight. The windscreen wipers wiped. The horn blared.

'That's *very* funny. We might as well take the rope off. If you get into any trouble, sound the horn.'

'Supposing there isn't a horn?'

'I'll follow *you*,' said Jack.

The next day I travelled a full thirty-five miles without the suspicion of a hitch. It was in that stretch of road which leads up from Wandsworth Bridge to the more dubious parts of Chelsea that there was a declivity in the surface. A manhole cover, no doubt. The monstrous front curtseyed in acknowledgement, but failed to return to the horizontal, and began to skate along the road, making the noise of a hundred washboards and throwing out a shower of sparks.

This time it was ho! for just a little north of the park.

'If I were you,' the Fiat agent said, 'I'd get rid of it.'

I didn't get rid of it. I found that I had discovered an entirely new and enticing form of motoring. For years, without noticing it, I had been reduced to an extremity of boredom by consistently arriving at my destination. Now I never did. I can't remember a single occasion on which that car failed to think up some novel form of breakdown. I never knew what was going to happen next, or where. In London streets, in lonely places, uphill, downhill, in traffic jams and the battle of the by-pass, the clutch would fail to engage, or else it would fail to disengage, or the brakes would become delightfully non-existent, or nothing would stop the engine running when I tried to turn it off, or would start it when I tried to turn it on. I drove with a

constant air of discovery. I had never had the slightest
idea that there were so many parts in a car which could
fail in such a lighthearted fashion. I was exalted. I
drove the local garage and the Fiat man up the wall
with my daily telephone calls for rescue from the most
improbable places. Some of them were very difficult
to describe. My daughter-in-law had found an ingenious way, on the map, of niggling to our house
through suburban roads, with the idea of avoiding the
Kingston By-pass. One disappeared from view somewhere in Morden or Merton, and emerged into
daylight again on the Chessington Road, near the Zoo.
At one point in this journey, I became aware of the
fact that one of the front wheels was obeying the
movements of the steering wheel. The other pointed
straight ahead. I hugged this idiosyncrasy to my heart,
but realized that obviously it would be dangerous to
continue. I had not the faintest idea where I was. I
might have been in Merton, Morden, Ewell, on the
outskirts of Epsom, Cheam, or Ashtead. I simply did
not know. In the distance I could see a pub, called The
Kingfisher. I decided the only thing to do was to ring
my daughter-in-law up, and ask her if she could place
me.

She is a great telephonist, and it was some time
before I could get through to her. After half a dozen or
so engaged signals, I finally made contact.

'Jessica.'

'Oh hullo! Where are you?'

'I was just going to ask you.'

'Don't you know?'

'No. I don't.'

'Why don't you?'

'The thing is that my car's broken down on your
special route.'

'Not again?'

'Yes. Rather. I was wondering if you could help me pinpoint the exact spot so that I could tell the garage where to find me.'

'How long have you been driving?'

'Oh, I should think about twenty minutes from your place.'

'Well, have you crossed the Epsom Road?'

'I think so. Two of them.'

'Oh!' she said. 'You must be near the seven lunatic asylums.'

'Oh really?'

'Just tell him you're near the seven lunatic asylums.'

'O.K.'

I rang off and got through to Hutchings at the Peaslake garage.

'I say. Could you possibly come and rescue me?'

'Where are you this time?'

'I'm near the seven lunatic asylums.'

There was a long pause.

'Are you pulling my leg?'

'No, no, my dear chap. I'm assured on the best authority that there are seven lunatic asylums.'

'Whose authority?'

'My daughter-in-law's.'

There was another of those long pauses.

'Just right of the Chessington Zoo. You can't miss them.'

'I'll do my best.'

'Thanks awfully. I'm in a pub called The King-fisher.'

'Stay where you are.'

'Don't worry.'

This was the determining moment when my daughter-in-law and her husband, my son, decided to

179

take matters in their own hands. They offered to buy
me a Bentley.

I found it surprisingly easy to get rid of the Fiat. It
was so flashy. I discovered a rather sombre, neat 'little
Bentley', a four-door fairly square-cut saloon, in not
very good condition. The man at Dorking, to whom I
showed it when I first obtained it, and who came for a
run in it, declared that it had some rather 'meaty
knocks'. It was extraordinarily comfortable within,
with armrests all round and the most delightful picnic
tables laid into the backs of the front seats. It had a
sunshine roof and a windscreen which opened when
you turned a little handle. You could obtain a blast of
air full in the face. This was marvellous on very hot
days. A Bentley is, of course, a Bentley, with or
without meaty knocks, and Albert, to whom I took it
for a vetting, assured me that it wouldn't break down.
It didn't.

Daily commuting to and from London gives an
awful bashing to a car. This thirty-year-old machine
carried me, with absolute accuracy and split-second
timing, between my house and my office with never
a falter. The effect was surprising at first after the
delicious vagaries of the Fiat. I cannot help wondering
how many of the cars which are thrust forth from the
factories today will be alive and running on the roads,
without any attention, in thirty years' time. We took
it down to Devonshire and it rushed up that hill from
Sidmouth, knocking aristocratically in top gear while
the rest of the traffic was grinding away in second.

I cannot remember who made the body but I think
it must have been Arthur Mulliner. It had that look.
There were others like it which I occasionally met on
my travels. I even saw the identical body behind a

Rolls-Royce radiator in a place eccentrically called Walberswick in Suffolk.

I was extremely grateful to my son and his wife for putting me once again on a footing of gentility. But I told you Bentleys brought me bad luck.

It was that damned publishing again.

I had taken a job, for the sake of the money. As far as I am concerned this is invariably fatal. I am constitutionally incapable of doing what any other man wants me to do. I will not take orders. The slightest suggestion on the part of an employer that I should do this or that drives me instantly to the precise contrary. I was very well treated indeed. I was given a beautiful office in Kensington Court where we shared the telephone line with the lady downstairs, who combined the arts of prostitution with the business of a procurist. Since the telephone was at my elbow on the desk I was always able to grab it before the lady downstairs had time to run from her bedroom or bidet. I overheard some very remarkable conversations.

'Oh, good afternoon. Your name has been given to me with very strong recommendations.'

Simpering noises.

'Could I possibly come and see you round about five o'clock this afternoon?'

'Yes, of course. Could you make that round about six? I rather want to get my hair done.'

'I er—I er—think I ought to warn you that I am rather the shy type.'

'Oh, that's all right. Do you prefer darkness?'

'What a good idea!'

Then there was a man who rang up and asked to speak to Tony.

'I want to speak to Tony.'

'Speaking.'

'No, no. I want to speak to Tony.'

'I am Tony.'

'Well you're the wrong one.'

'There's nobody else here of that name.'

'Yes, there is. It's a girl.'

'Oh Lord. Sorry. Hold on.'

I did the hook-rattling which in the end usually produced the lady below. But this time a succulent, flatulent child's voice answered.

'Nigel! Darling!'

'Yes. Well, about this business of going down to see my mother—'

'But darling! Of course I'm going down to see your mother.'

'I don't believe it's actually necessary.'

'Nigel, don't be so silly! I must go and show myself to your mother. Surely she'll want to see the girl to whom her son is engaged.'

The man's voice took on a tinge of misery.

'Are we engaged?'

'Darling, you *know* we are! I'll take her an enormous bunch of flowers.'

'She's got flowers.'

'Well, chocolates then. I shall take an enormous box of chocolates.'

'Probably make her sick.'

'Darling Nigel. I do love you! You know I do! Don't you love me?'

'Well, in a way I suppose I do. But I don't see why we should bother Mother about all this. I mean, supposing we change our minds?'

'Darling, you're in a funny mood today. Don't forget I've got it in writing. You'll feel better when you get down to Gloucestershire.'

I wonder how much it cost him to get out of that one.

Then, not on the telephone this time, there was a staggeringly beautiful girl with a veil across her eyes, who burst in breathlessly and said, 'I've come to report.'

Then she saw the look on my face.

'Oh! Isn't this the Iranian Embassy?'

'No, it isn't. But you can report to me if you like.'

She was most attractively confused.

'It's the North end of the square. There's a big shield over the door.'

'Oh dear!' she said and turned first her head, and then her whole body, and melted away.

'That's funny,' as Jack Hutchings would have said. But it didn't make for successful publishing. After about six months I became gloomily aware that my proprietor was not absolutely pleased with what was going on in Kensington Court. I could see it in the whole cast of his body which became increasingly bird-like. And then one day, the blow fell. He very seldom came to my office. Naturally I was expected to go to his. On this occasion, he turned up in Kensington Court and I immediately suspected the worst. We talked about publishing for some time and then when I saw him out he said, 'That old Bentley of yours. Wouldn't you like to trade it in for a new car?'

I knew what that meant. He was being kind.

'I'd be prepared to make up the difference on something really new, providing you aren't too extravagant.'

'That's terribly nice of you.'

'I just like to keep everybody happy, that's all.'

'Well I must say it's frightfully generous.'

Three weeks later it happened. The sack. It was perfectly justified, of course. Nobody ought ever to employ me. And I ought never to drive a Bentley.

So I went to the Motor Show. And there my eye fell

on that enchanting little absurdity, the Goggomobil.
It was absolutely minute, and the bodywork by Ghia
was, as the advertisements were saying, 'as pretty as a
picture'.

Though I like large and imposing vehicles to boost
my ego, I also have a passion for very small things. I
like to carry everything I could possibly need in my
pockets. For years I carried a Minox camera with me
wherever I went, which is about three inches long and
half an inch wide. I also have the smallest radio in the
world, or so Sony tell me. I even carry a pair of very
small binoculars in my hip pocket. Isn't that absurd?

The little Goggomobil wound its way into my heart
at once. And when I found that it had a push-button
electric gear-box, I'm afraid I fell. As Oscar Wilde said,
'The only thing I cannot resist is temptation.'

That night as I went home in the Bentley, I overtook one of those things in the general region of the
Ace of Spades. It was making a tremendous roaring
and it was scudding along at a considerable rate of
knots. I thought to myself that if I was going to be the
possessor of such a fascinating midget, I had better
show it once and for all, and indeed for the last time,
what a Bentley could do. So, as I say, I passed it.

There used to be lights at the Ace of Spades instead
of the present roundabout, and when they went red he
came alongside. When they changed, he shot away from
me. I could hardly believe my eyes. I trod on the old
Bentley and passed him again, but the sound of his
roar pursued me. It pursued me all along the Chessington Road to Leatherhead, round the Leatherhead By-
pass, and it was only on the down stretch from the
By-pass to the Dorking road that I lost him. Later I
knew why.

184   I had the greatest difficulty in persuading the Goggo-

mobil concessionaire to allow me £100 on the Bentley. In the end hysterical tears did the trick. I crawled into my dainty dwarf and had a most amusing time showing the rest of the London traffic what I could do. That electric gear-box was an absolute delight. I found that I kept my hand hanging by one finger from the top of the facia and used the others to play it like a typewriter. Using the buttons fast, the speed of getaway from standstill left everybody gasping. The game really had to be played from the inside. There was nearly always room for the little Goggo to creep up on the left and then 'dab', 'dab', 'dab', and away you went. The engine was a two-cylinder two-stroke which, as I am sure you know, has only seven moving parts. It was tucked away low down at the back and was quite vibrationless, so that the man behind you was much more aware of it than you were yourself.

That Leatherhead By-pass ends in quite a fast slope, down which the traffic sweeps with very little throttle. I swept down it myself at about 50 with practically no throttle at all, when disaster struck. There was a noise like the screech of tyres. Harking back to it, I think perhaps there *was* a squeal of tyres. What's more, they were my tyres. The car was slewing all over the road. People were jamming on their brakes. All I knew was that both back wheels had ceased to rotate, and when I finally came to rest and tried the starter, there was a clonk and silence.

Will somebody kindly explain to me why the manufacturers of two-stroke engines, whether for motorcars, bicycles, lawnmowers, hedge-trimmers, chain saws or outboard motors, play this absurd pre-Raphaelite game of mixing the oil with the petrol? I am aware, of course, that the crank case is under compression and cannot, therefore, have a lot of oil floating in it; but is there any reason on earth why they shouldn't use the eminently satisfactory system of dry-sump lubrication, practised in the pre-war Aston Martin? There is none. It is obscurantism. And the net result is that if you find yourself travelling fast with very little throttle, you are at the same time travelling fast with very little oil. The blasted Goggo had seized solid. The only thing to do was to coast into the ditch, smoke two cigarettes, one after the other, and wait for the expansion noises and the blast of heat to yield to the cooling breeze.

During the twenty minutes I gave it, it seemed to me that the problem was so deep-seated as to be insoluble. If I took that incline more slowly there would be even *less* oil getting to the cylinders. The only course offered to me, it seemed, was not to use the Leatherhead By-pass at all, but to drive through the centre of the town. It seemed to me that it was a pretty miserable contraption which dictated its own route.

After twenty minutes or so, when the only sound was that of cars sweeping by, the engine restarted meekly, and I went upon my way.

Jack Hutchings, to whom I put the problem, thought that the only way to overcome it was to drive down that particular section of road flat out.

'Don't be absurd,' I said. 'I want to live for quite a number of years yet.'

'Try a richer mixture. It should be all right at about twelve to one.'

So we tried a richer mixture. It worked, but at the expense of emitting as choking a cloud of blue smoke as the old sleeve-valve Daimler. Daimlers were allowed to do this. People were rude about the Goggo to the point of embarrassment. It became almost impossible to start in the mornings, unless one took out both plugs and wiped away the oil and soot. I went back to the old recommended mixture, and developed a technique, using the electric gear-box, of pushing it along fairly hard, switching in neutral, switching back to top, and carrying on in a series of ungainly and dangerous swoops. It was only after I had got rid of the car in disgust, and went back to the Motor Show, which was still running, that an old hand at two-strokes gave me the answer to the difficulty. It was really very simple. But it came too late. You motored quite normally in normal circumstances; but, if you came to a stretch of road which looked as if it might bring on a seizure, you gave the engine a generous helping of choke.

The problem now was money. My salary was gone from me and, since my former boss had stumped up a few hundreds to mitigate the blow, I could hardly return to him for more. I needed the cheapest thing on four wheels. And the cheapest thing at that particular period in time came from behind the Iron Curtain at an artificially lowered price in a desperate attempt to obtain foreign currency. It was, in fact, a most curiously shaped Czechoslovakian export called the Skoda.

In a communistic, proletarian sort of way, it was a very practical, utilitarian sort of car. That is to say it went along with four people inside it, sitting on rather high comfortable seats. It had the most all-embracing tool kit I have ever beheld. It had a very odd and unenviable bulge about nine inches high, running all round, between the waistline and the window sills. It made one think of the antimacassars and the aspidistras reputed to be among the furnishings of the Russian jet-liner. The whole thing was painted an obscene butcher's blue, and it would pull down to five miles an hour in top gear.

I don't really feel myself in prole vehicles. The engine was fitted with painstaking tightness. It took nearly 20,000 miles before it began to move at all freely and by that time everything made of rubber had deteriorated disastrously. The tyres were bald, the battery was split, and all the little things like wiper blades and grommets and pedal pads and windscreen sealings and so on were very much the worse for wear. I suppose that, in spite of all the five-year plans, the Iron Curtain countries were short of certain raw materials.

There was a thief who assisted in this process. Unless it comes to me as a perquisite or bonus on a second-hand deal, I never have a wireless in a car. As you may have guessed, I am interested in cars. I like to listen to them. I use my ears very much in driving. I hear the man behind me make up his mind to overtake, as well as see him in the mirror. At blind turnings I always cock an ear to warn me of oncoming traffic. I often startle myself by confirming a suspicion that there is something travelling too fast round the next bend and, as I haven't any sixth senses, I must have heard it. The very last thing I want is this facility to be taken away from me in favour of 'The Archers'. But I did leave my small transistor in the Skoda one day and some ingenious person, in broad daylight, inserted a hook on the end of a piece of bent wire through the rubber moulding on the quarter lights, and undid the door handle from the inside. I was sorry to lose my little radio, which the insurance company immediately paid for, thus depriving me of my no-claim bonus. And when I got home I found myself a piece of wire, and spent a happy hour trying various folds and permutations with no success whatever. I

can recommend it as a most unrewarding pastime for a

dull afternoon, but must also warn you that if you are
the proud owner of a Skoda the rain water will enter
freely ever after.

I cannot think what possessed me. Obviously I am
groovy. I get into ruts. After trundling about for the
best part of a year in that vitriol-blue, goitrous, lower-
middle-class equipage, I changed my Skoda for another.

It was purely on account of the bulge. I read a
report in *The Motor* of a journalist visiting Prague,
which he illustrated with a photograph of a drophead
Skoda taken against a background of Saint Wenceslas
Square. No bulge.

One dies a thousand deaths in the cause of art. I
effected the swap with cash adjustment and when
it was delivered to my door, I was forced to close my
eyes. Not only was it painted an obscene yellow, but
the coupé part was obscenely too far forwards. The
boot was about two feet longer than the bonnet, and
this produced a very unrehearsed effect which I find
difficult to describe. Did it look like an eland? Or like
a woman on her stomach, peering over a low stone
wall? Or was it simply that the cart was put before the
horse? At all events, something had to be done about
this immediately. The car was perfectly all right when
the hood was in the open position, but the moment it
was closed, it began that extraordinary questing of the
hooded cobra. So I went to a hood repairer and got
him to make me some extra long hood sticks at the
back so as to bring the whole erection two feet further
to the rear. It was while we were working on this that
we discovered that by cutting away a lot of cardboard
the back seat could also be moved a couple of feet, so
that one could actually sit on it. This was a great
improvement. But the hood looked, if anything, more
extraordinary than before. The blind section at the

side was now two feet longer than the window, and, apart from the fact that the occupants of the rear seat could not now see out of the car, the whole contrivance now had something of the barmy appearance of that Lotus with the Renault engine in the middle. There was really nothing for it but to buy some very warm clothes and treat it as an open car.

I am forced to admit that this peculiar automobile, obviously designed for the playboy-bureaucrat or the more sporting members of the secret police, travelled really rather well. The engine had been hotted up considerably so that it showed something in the region of sixty-five brake horsepower. It had definite punch. It would slog manfully on its four high-compression cylinders. At the same time it would contrive a well-managed 70 with no sound but the flapping of that frightful hood. By this time the 70 mph speed limit had been imposed. This has always seemed to me a very reasonable state of affairs and I have made a point of scrupulously kowtowing to it, except on one occasion which I shall tell you about in a moment.

I drove that car, shivering with cold, for quite some time, but not having had any leanings towards membership of the Politburo it never struck me as a car with which one could really identify oneself. It could never be an expression of one's own personality. To use the cliché, it wasn't really *me*.

So one day it happened that I went to a cocktail party and met a young man.

'Is that comic thing yours outside?' he asked.

'Yes, it is.'

'Looks like the tunnel of love.'

'It's better with the hood down.'

'Why don't you get Hutchings to flog it to somebody

and buy my SP 250?'

The SP 250 is what was known in its earlier years as the Daimler Dart. The adrenalin level began to rise.

'Do you want to sell her?'

'I like something much more hairy. It's too damned gentlemanly for me. I've ordered a TR2.'

'Could I let Hutchings have a look at it?'

'Of course. He shall have it in the morning.'

I gulped a considerable quantity of champagne.

I made my rounds. A retired general, a Director of the Bank of England, the widow of a fashionable London doctor. It has always amused me and sometimes horrified me to tot up the secret wealth stashed away in this one little Surrey village. I don't think it is possible for one agreeable grey-haired lady to live by herself in a nice house, with an acre or so of garden, a small car, a gardener once a week, champagne parties and a woman who 'does', on a capital of less than £80,000. If you multiply this by a hundred and add to it the capital of the really rich ones who live in the Georgian houses, surrounded by their fields, the total must be formidable. People talk about the balance of payments, unemployment on the Clyde, the collapse of an Empire, the need to go into Europe, but the hidden reserves of this country must make it still one of the richest in the world. Yet to drive through Peaslake, and come upon the one little shop, see small boys wheeling about on bicycles, the butcher cleaving meat to someone in a tattered Land Rover, three patient people in the bus shelter, and a 1938 Alvis, one Vauxhall and one Ford outside the Trust House Inn, and you would never suspect.

I make this digression to produce the same effect as the cocktail party had upon my own mind. I hope I made all the proper noises and said the proper things. But underneath it all, I could think of nothing but the

SP 250 with its eight-cylinder engine, waiting for me
if I wanted it. I slept like a log after all that champagne,
dreaming of Daimlers and Delages and my old
Phantom Continental, since which I had never owned
a proper car. The next morning, bright and early, I
was down at the garage. And there she was. Black,
thank goodness. It had a canvas hood, with side
pieces cut out of it at the back, which I didn't altogether like, but Hutchings told me there was also a
detachable top. He knew the car, having sold it, and
serviced it ever since.

'Can I take the driver's seat?'

'Go ahead.'

It was rather like lying in bed, with one's feet out at
full stretch. There were a great many dials telling you
everything you could possibly want to know. The
speedometer read 32,000 miles. Hutchings closed the
door and a strange sensation flowed through me. The
car fitted. The pedals were at one's toes. The gear lever
at the fingers of the left hand. The steering wheel
nicely into the chest (I hate that long arm business).
Despite the overall lowness of the car, there was room
to wear a top hat. The windscreen was on the level
with one's eyes.

Hutchings got in beside me with great difficulty. He
was a heavy man and the secret of getting in and out of
a car like this is to sit down first and then swing the
legs in, or alternatively swing the legs out and then
stand up. If you try to move one foot in at a time,
you'll never make it.

'Starter?'

'On the key.'

I turned it. With no plonks or clanks of any description the engine began to hiss quietly to itself. This is
how a cat must feel when it's stroked. If I knew how,

I should have purred. All I could do was to swallow
back my emotion by gulping twice. The feel of a really
civilized piece of machinery under one was something
I had missed for five years.

'Where shall we go?'

'Stane Street?'

It was a Roman road.

'O.K.'

I reversed on to the garage forecourt. I shoved in
what I thought was second gear, and the car moved
off.

'You're in top, old cock.'

'May as well stay there now.'

A dab on the accelerator and we swooped away. My
daughter, who drove the car quite a bit later, had the
right words to describe the feel of it. She said, 'Just
feather the pedal and the car slides away from under
you.' We took the steepest of the five roads climbing
out of Peaslake. Things like Skodas require second
gear. We snaked up it unobtrusively in top and when
we levelled out, the Daimler's swooping motion
exhibited itself. I felt like a swallow. A dab on the
accelerator or a dab on the brake seemed to produce
swirls and whorls. When we got to Stane Street, I
thought I'd run her up to 70 mph just to see how things
went. So I put my foot down. I couldn't get the
needle much further than about 65.

'Steady on,' said Hutchings, reaching for the door
handle.

'Why doesn't it do 70?'

'You're looking at the rev counter.' And, by golly, so
I was. We were nudging 125 mph.

If Daimlers were as well made as Rolls-Royces, that
little car would have been the last car I ever owned. It
was small enough to do twenty-five miles to the gallon.

Small enough indeed to be frequently mistaken from
behind for something on the lines of the Hillman Imp.
With that wonderful engine under the bonnet, putting
out 140 horsepower, its power-weight ratio was in a
class, almost, of its very own. You caressed the
accelerator rather than put your foot on it. It would
trickle along to 10 mph with all its power impulses
still overlapping, and the merest touch would send it
leaping forward from 10 to 20 to 30 to 40 mph, taking
about two seconds for each step. Its manners were
impeccable. The engine turned exactly like a turbine.
The steering was as heavy as lead, and as solid as a
rock. Its springing was a little sturdy at low speeds,
but smoothed out wonderfully when we sped. Only
once again did we attempt any sort of high speed, and
that was coming back from Devonshire when my wife
was sleeping by my side on that invitingly straight
piece of empty road across the edges of Salisbury Plain,
between Puddlecombe and Blandford Forum. We
touched 95 for a few seconds and my wife never woke.

The Police used these cars until they wore them out.
This had two rather nice results. It made the Police
friendlier; and it made all the other motorists extremely respectful in restricted areas, particularly in
the dark where my bare head was not immediately
apparent.

I never thought, of course, that this was to be the last
of the real Daimler Daimlers. The car had so many
merits that it seemed inconceivable that it could be
dropped. In towns it was elaborately unobtrusive and
polite. Its acceleration, particularly in second gear,
was like a blast-off from the pad. In some ways its
characteristics at low speed were the most attractive
of the lot. On a fine summer evening in country lanes
194 one could waft along to 25 mph or so, enjoying the

flicker of the sunshine and the twitter of the birds, without any thought of a gear change. If one came across anything less steep than an incline of one in six, the only difficulty was that it became a matter of extreme irritation to other motorists, whose four-cylinder engines of half the size but pulling cars of twice the weight were really undriveable in hilly country at speeds of anything less than 40. On my journeys from London I found that, after sitting over the wheel for the first thirty miles of main road, it was pleasant to turn aside at a place like Effingham and saunter through the woods at bicycling pace. Before half another mile had been covered, there would be a long queue of five or six cars behind me, not hooting exactly, but showing every desire to pass. The only thing to do in these circumstances was to stop in a wide place and wave them all on, or else put on a spurt myself, and leave them to it.

But the Daimler Company was bought up by that Sir William Lyons who used to make Austin Swallows. In no time at all, the SP 250 sidled out of the lists, and the V-eight engine, with lower gear ratios, was installed within the banana-like outlines of the Jaguar. Now even that has been dropped, and the Daimler only remains as a radiator, a D on the wheels, and a crinkly treatment of the back light. I read that Jaguars have made a twelve-cylinder motor. If they had only put it behind a proper Daimler radiator as the Daimler Double Six, and had resisted the temptation to instal it in Jaguars as well, that would have gone some way to restoring the most famous name in motoring to its proper place.

When the figure of 32,000 on the clock had risen to 82,000, there were definite signs of wear. The first gear, which I never used, made horrid grating noises if someone else did. I had to renew things on the steering such as toggle joints. And the engine began to emit clouds of smoke.

This interfered with one of my best tricks on the By-pass. In gay and happy mood, I would insert my second gear at the lights, wait for the change, and then go straight through to 60, leaving the rest of the pack about a quarter of a mile behind. Caddish I know. But now when I tried this the other cars became completely blotted from view, and I realized that this practice had got to stop.

In fact, something had to be done. I couldn't pick up a later model because they had stopped making them. There wasn't anything so good remotely near to it in price. And then one day, idly searching through the second-hand columns of *The Motor*, I came across an advertisement from some chap in Bournemouth who had a model of the same age, but with automatic gears, and only 32,000 'guaranteed mileage' on the clock. I immediately got on the telephone to him and invited myself down to Bournemouth the following day. When I turned up at about half past twelve, he showed me his car, which was a great deal shinier and newer-looking than mine, and then bought me an extremely good lunch. Over the brandy we settled on a price differential of £200. This was probably rather a lot, but I thought that if I bought 50,000 miles of Daimler motoring for £200, it was a pretty good bargain. So I came home in her.

Two days later, I received a letter from a parson—at least I suppose he was a parson because his address was The Vicarage—demanding to know what on earth had persuaded me to part with such a beautiful car with only 12,000 miles on the clock. In an absent-minded moment someone must have hit the speedometer a very hard blow during the night.

This was a very disturbing discovery because, naturally, it made me look at my own speedometer, and to examine the brake pedals and the carpets and the general state of the car. I came to the conclusion that the 32,000 was genuine. Now I know it was because I ran that one up to nearly the 80,000 mark and there was nary a sign of smoke. Only a little piston slap and a bit of clatter from the cam-followers. That's the trouble with the V-eight engine. The pistons are lying on their sides and they wear topsidedly.

I still have my car, and I propose to keep it. We get on very well together, so well, in fact, that when I read in the paper that Jaguars were dropping the V-eight engine altogether, I decided that the time had come to spend some money on it. So I took it up to Daimler's, miles away in Cricklewood or somewhere, and they renewed every piece of it. It cost more than the entire second-hand price of the car. But in my way I feel I have outwitted the restructurers and the streamliners. I have a perfectly brand new SP 250. I expect we shall see each other out.

I wonder how much longer I shall be able to go crashing about the roads. I am really a thirties man. That was my best period, as well as the golden age of cars. It was the time when they built beautiful houses and furnished them in good taste. They threw the wallpapers out of the windows, finished the walls in eggshell blue and planted eighteenth-century furniture about in all the right places. John Betjeman calls it 'the period of ghastly good taste'. I feel people beginning to look upon me as a nonagenarian eccentric. I walk the streets in the suits of the thirties, with the broad shoulder and the slim hips and the permanent turn-ups. In winter, at least, I wear a homburg tilted rather

rakishly to one side and without a bulge of hair
protruding from behind it. My overcoat reaches down
halfway between my knee and the ankle. I like the
music of the thirties and find it impossible to listen
to anything later than Glenn Miller. I think it was our
most civilized period. We had all the conveniences we
have today, except perhaps television, and although we
were heading for a war we didn't know it.

Now we are getting well into the seventies, and one
of these days, if I am not careful, I shall find myself
going the way of the Freestone and Webb Rolls-
Royces, the Hispano-Suizas, the Delages, the
Mercedes, the Duesenbergs, the Isotta Fraschinis. I
shall be in good company.

But I am not careful. I told you many pages ago of
how I once crashed into the tailboard of a stationary
lorry. Last Sunday I did precisely the same thing. I
had just got my Daimler back, with its beautiful new
engine, and was on my way home from Buckingham-
shire where I had been taking tea with a friend of mine
who runs a two-litre Rover. Why do they put so much
advertising on the back of these cars? 'TC', 'De-
Luxe,' 'Discs,' '2000', 'GT'. One of the nicest things
about the SP 250 is that there is absolutely nothing
written on the back except the letter 'D'. There could be
plenty: 'V-eight', '140 BHP', 'TC', 'Discs All Round'.

Ah well! As I say, I was returning from Bucking-
hamshire and had arrived safely and expeditiously at
Guildford. There is a 'give way' sign there where you
break into the Aldershot Road, which comes down
quite steeply at an acute angle from the right. There
was that same little queue of cars waiting for a gap in
the traffic before moving out. As before, we emerged
one by one and moved up to keep station. At last there
was one young woman in front of me in a pre-war

Austin. She moved off. I stuck my head out of the side
window and saw a lorry rattling down very fast with a
gap behind it.

'After that lorry,' I said to myself.

As it passed I put my foot on the floor, and with a
whoosh of acceleration went straight in to the back of the
pre-war Austin which had only moved about two yards.

This isn't senility. It's a blank spot in my imagination. Twenty years ago, when I was a young man, I
had done precisely the same thing outside Dorking
Station. Thirty years before that when I was a mere
boy, I had done it again, this time on a bicycle, on
which I ploughed into the back of a stationary water
cart. I passed out on that occasion and came to in the
arms of an unusually beautiful Jewess. Evidently I
have a childish and confident belief that traffic on my
own side of the road can be relied upon to move along
the road, rather than remain stationary.

If things go on as they are, these shunts are going to
become so common that the thunder and roar of
traffic will be dispensed with, and the only sounds will
be the tinkle of glass and the scratching of ballpoints
exchanging particulars for the insurance companies.
The four great companies, Ford, BMC, Chrysler and
General Motors spewing out material for subsequent
junkyards had better take warning. One of these days,
quite soon now, much sooner than many people think,
sooner, I firmly believe, than when half the motorways
now projected are finished, the motorcar is going to
make itself obsolete. We shall take to the air, of course.
That will be the day. I shall enjoy that. When these
things happen, they happen very quickly. Look at the
disappearance of steam. Look at the disappearance of
the railways themselves. If you want to go further back
look at the clearance of the canals. Only two or three

months ago there stood in the front hall of the Royal
Automobile Club a charming little autogiro with
chromium-plated vanes which could be bought, if I
remember, for something in the region of £1,800. The
autogiro is no good because, like the ordinary aero-
plane, it needs a runway to take off. But a neat little
helicopter could undoubtedly be produced in large
numbers for a price of that sort. If there is to be any
traffic density in the air, the principle of that giant
rotating thing, so admirably adapted to sawing off
objects which come within its reach, will have to be
abandoned in favour of ducted fans. I am prepared to
bet fifteen new pence that in another fifteen years the
roads will show signs of becoming deserted. Then all
the little tin boxes will be piled helter-skelter in unattractive places where the rain can turn them into
rust and the grass will begin to grow on the roads of
England.

INDEX OF CARS *Italics indicate illustrations*